The Star Wars Rings

The Hidden Structure Behind the Story

Tomas Pueyo Brochard

For Alonso and Olivia, my own little Luke and Leia.

Table of Contents

Introduction

As *Star Wars Episode VII – The Force Awakens* hit theaters in December of 2015, fans across the world anxiously awaited what was to come. Everybody had the same question: will this movie be as good as the originals? Or would it follow the same terrible formula of George Lucas's prequels, riddled with bad acting, trite plots, and ridiculous new elements?

Thankfully, JJ Abrams, the man behind *The Force Awakens*, showed some creativity – and mercy – and created the best Star Wars experience since *Episode VI – The Return of the Jedi*. Audiences raved about *The Force Awakens*: back to the roots of Star Wars! No more Jar Jar Binks! No more whining Hayden Christensen!

Abrams steered away from the prequels and squarely into *A New Hope*'s original content. Maybe he steered a little too far. In fact, if you walk through each movie scene by scene, they feel like the same film. Both have a droid that contains a secret: R2-D2 and BB-8. Both portray a young person living in a broken family in a desert world: Luke Skywalker and Rey. In both cases, the hero is compelled to join the good guys fighting against the bad guys. In both cases, the hero faces a representative force of evil clothed in black: Darth Vader and Kylo Ren. Each movie features a sphere that can destroy planets: the Death Star and Starkiller Base.

"What is wrong with JJ?" some asked. "Why is it more of the same? Does he have no creativity?" Those people were the same ones that thought the prequels – Episodes I through III – were too reiterative, lacked creativity, or were just plain bad.

Why did Abrams decide to create a story so similar to the original Episode IV? Why so many parallels? Why reuse so many motifs? And why were the prequels criticized for the exact same reason?

People were busy shunning the movies and criticizing them, but they didn't dwell on why the filmmakers decided to make the movies so similar. If they had, they would have discovered that George Lucas and JJ Abrams were not mindlessly repeating themes. They would have seen that the story of a youngster with a knack for piloting and robots living on a desert planet is the same for Rey and Luke, but also Anakin. They would have seen that it's not just Episode IV and VII that look alike, but that there are also similarities to Episode I, George Lucas's 1999 prequel. They would have noticed that Episodes I through VI are a complete arc for Anakin, and Episodes IV through VI are just half the arc for Luke. They would have noticed that many shots of Episode I mirror nearly perfectly similar shots in Episode VI.

A critical look reveals that George Lucas and JJ Abrams were very thoughtful in each theme, scene, and shot of every movie. They built a blueprint for all the movies, from the high-level story down to the minute details.

This book is about that blueprint. It's about the map that makes sense of all the Star Wars movies. It explains the method behind the original trilogy; why three movies, why George Lucas chose the scenes he used. Why the ending was meant to be. Why the prequel starts the same way as the original trilogy, why it ends with Anakin Skywalker turning to the Dark Side, with the Empire defeating the Republic. With this book, you will discover the movies all over again, enjoying the filmmakers' every decision from a movie connoisseur's vantage point.

What's more, once you understand the blueprint, you'll be able to use it yourself. You will be able to predict much of what will happen in Episodes VIII and IX. You will be able to enjoy the new filmmakers' every decision because they will make sense, and you'll enjoy the surprises even more, because they'll resolve many of the remaining creative choices.

More importantly, you will understand why they built the blueprint the way they did, so you can build your own blueprint for your stories.

But to explain the blueprint, we first need to know its building blocks, how it's made. There's a method to crafting complex blueprints for stories. If we don't understand these storytelling building blocks, we can't interpret the full blueprint.

The good thing is that it's both easy and useful to understand these building blocks of storytelling. They are the same for all stories.

For example, have you ever heard a story where an ordinary boy is approached by someone magical who tells him he has superpowers? Someone who helps him grow until he is barely ready to confront evil, but he does anyway, and saves the world? *Star Wars? Harry Potter? The Matrix? Lord of the Rings? Avatar?*

Ever since the dawn of time, humans have told stories: love stories, hero stories, buddy stories, featuring monsters, superheroes, detectives... There are millions of stories, and thousands of ways to tell them.

The most successful stories, the ones that really pull you in, follow a similar structure. A protagonist wants something badly, but faces an obstacle to get it. The conflict is resolved by confronting the obstacle.

Every now and then, we stumble upon a special story. It doesn't just move us; it grabs our senses, grips our brains, and glues us to our seats. It transports us from our daily lives into fantastic worlds we don't want to leave.

This is the type of story that inspires us, defines our future, and changes the way we think. Stories like this survive the test of time and transcend borders, stories like *Star Wars*, the *Harry Potter* series or *Lord of the Rings*, but also Homer's *Iliad*, the Bible, or the Koran.

All these stories are somewhat alike, containing variations of the same theme, like different verses with the same rhyme. That's because they all follow the same structure. They all have a blueprint, and all their blueprints are alike. If you analyze these stories' structures and deeply understand them, how they're built and what hidden patterns they follow, you can create amazing stories of your own, or even predict the elements of existing stories that are yet to come.

That is what this book will enable you to do. In the first part, you will learn storytelling structures. These basic building blocks will enable us to examine more and more complex structures, culminating with the most complex structure in the book: the Ring Structure. This is the structure that stories like Star Wars have used as a blueprint.

In the second part of the book, we will use everything we've learned and apply it to Star Wars. We'll deconstruct its blueprint into its building blocks to understand how it's structured and why it works so well. Then, we'll rebuild the blueprint, following the Ring Structure. That will help us predict what will happen in the rest of the saga, in Episodes VIII and IX.

Chapter 1 will look at the main story structure types. In Chapter 2, we will analyze the Ring structure. It's the structure of Star Wars, but also corresponds to Harry Potter or parts of the Bible. Part II, which applies all our learnings to Star Wars, starts with Chapter 3, which demonstrates how the original trilogy of Star Wars IV, V and VI follows a Ring Structure. Chapter 4 extends the Ring Structure theory to Star Wars Episodes I through VI. Chapter 5 shows how Episode VII also fits into a Ring Structure and how that knowledge could have helped predict many elements of that movie. Finally, in Chapter 6 we will use the Ring Theory to predict Episodes VIII and IX.

Before I jump into the meat of the book, here are a couple of useful tips about Star Wars. You can read this book without having watched the movies. That said... What are you doing? Stop right now and go watch them! Do you really want to read a book about a story without knowing the story? Go! I'll be waiting here.

If you have watched the movies but are a bit hazy, or you haven't watched them all, you might want to quickly read the appendix, where I include a summary of Episodes I through VII. If you are very well acquainted with Star Wars, you can just jump to Chapter 1. If you're well-versed in both storytelling structure and Star Wars, you can just jump to Part II. Finally, if you don't care at all about storytelling structure and just want to get on with Star Wars, jump to Part II.

Throughout the book, I will be using SW4 to refer to Star Wars Episode IV, SW5 for Episode V, and so on. I will refer to the Original Trilogy— the movies originally created by George Lucas at the end of the 1970s and beginning of 1980s—as Episodes 4 through 6. The Prequel Trilogy refers to Episodes 1 through 3, also created by Lucas, at the end of the 1990s and the beginning of 2000s. The Sequel Trilogy refers to the new Episodes VII through IX, which started in December 2015 with JJ Abrams's Episode 7 – The Force Awakens.

All these movies seem to be tied just by their existence in the same universe, and maybe some similarities. In fact, they all follow a grand pattern. It's hard to see the structure just by watching the movies: your eyes can deceive you. Don't trust them. Once you understand how the Star Wars blueprint follows a Ring Structure, you won't be able to unsee it. Follow the path of the Ring Structure, and you will master the Star Wars story.

PART I

STORYTELLING STRUCTURES

Chapter 1: The Building Blocks of Stories

The hunters listen carefully around the fire. Their friend is narrating how the high grass was moving just before the lion jumped out of it and attacked the herd of antelope near the river. The hunters put aside everything they were doing to listen. Time has stopped.

They are listening so attentively because stories are irresistible for humans. Stories are like a drug for our brains. We like them so much that we make up stories even when there aren't any. Why are stories so compelling? Because they helped our ancestors learn things they needed for their survival, like our hunters above: What area should they avoid if they don't want an unlucky meeting with a lion? How can they read the high grass to predict an attack? Should the village band together to hunt the lion down?

For millions of years, we've evolved to listen to stories to learn about our environments, predict what's next, and improve our lives. Because most stories came in the format of a person learning from a problem they faced, humans have become especially attuned to what we call stories: a protagonist wants something really, really badly, but faces an obstacle to get it. When those stories were told, they usually contained vital information for their lives, so they grew accustomed to listening to them carefully.

Let's go back to our hunters. They are listening to a story where there is a protagonist, the other hunter that narrates the story. He wants something really badly: to survive the lion. There is an obstacle (or antagonistic force, or more simply, antagonist): the lion. The structure of "The hunter wants to survive but the lion threatens him" is "The protagonist wants something badly but can't get it because of the antagonist".

Some stories are more compelling than others. The story of a neighbor who wanted to clean his lawn of stones but was too lazy to do it isn't very interesting. You still have a protagonist (the neighbor), something he wants (to clean the lawn of stones) and an antagonist (his laziness). Yet it's not as interesting as the hunter's story. Why? What he wants is not something he really really wants: if he did, he would just clean the lawn. And the antagonist is not very strong: laziness is relatively easy to overcome.

Let's take another example. Imagine the same village of hunter-gatherers. Bok is the strongest hunter of the tribe, the alpha male. He rules the group with his partner, the alpha female Kana. But Kana is attracted to one of the young males of the tribe, Lambo. They fall in love. They escape. Bok, furious, chases them, finds them, and attacks Lambo. Lambo defends himself, but he's no match for Bok, who pounds on him with all his rage. He's about to strike the final blow when his companion, Kana, strikes him from behind with a stone, killing him. Lambo and Kana become the new ruling couple of the tribe.

Why is this second story so much more interesting? It contains vital information for a member of the tribe: there's a new alpha male, Lambo. But he is young, weak, and doesn't respect existing relationships. Kana, the alpha female, has much more power than one could have guessed. She's also not trustworthy. She lets her passions drive her decisions and betrayed her previous companion. Bok, the previous alpha male, was violent and possessive; but Lambo is not. The dynamics of the tribe are about to change...

All this information is very important for a member of the tribe to learn. The people who evolved to take interest in such a story had an advantage over others.

The themes of passion, violence, and betrayal make the story compelling. But the themes alone don't achieve that. If the story was just "the alpha female and the beta male got rid of the alpha male", it wouldn't be so interesting because it would omit most of the relevant information.

The structure of the story itself is key to making it compelling. There are clear protagonists, Kana and Lambo. They really, really want something: to love each other and survive. There's a very clear antagonist: Bok.

The story of a protagonist, his want, and his antagonist unfolds like a math problem: there's a goal, an obstacle, and a solution. The goal is for the protagonist to obtain his want, the obstacle is the antagonist, and the solution is how the story unfolds.

Storytelling is really just the traditional way of teaching problem-solving. It happens to be the only format our ancestors could use to share their experience with others, the way they could learn from one another and avoid the same problems. Obviously, the humans who were most compelled by stories were the ones who learned the most from other people's stories. They became more experienced. They could survive longer and have more kids, and those kids would inherit their love for stories. We've probably evolved to love stories because they were the best way to learn from other people's experiences in ancient times.

Initially, storytellers didn't know the formal rules of storytelling; they intuitively learned what constitutes a good story. But, over the centuries, our knowledge of what makes a good story has been evolving. Not every story has the same structure, but all the good ones use the same building blocks, rooted in our evolutionary craving for stories. By analyzing these building blocks, we can understand how to create amazing stories, and once we understand how amazing stories are made, we can start appreciating the immensely ambitious story structure that Star Wars follows.

The Shapes of Stories

Basic Structure

Even if you've never written a story, you can recognize one in a few seconds. You might not be able to articulate what makes it a story, but you know a story when you see or hear it. A story has a Setup, a Confrontation, and a Resolution.

It starts with the Setup, the part that we've focused on previously: a protagonist who lives a normal life until something happens to change it. That makes him really want to resolve the situation, but he's blocked from doing so by the obstacle: the antagonistic force. In our previous story, the setup is that Bok and Kana are together initially, but Kana and Lambo fall in love. In other famous stories: Little Red Riding Hood wants to bring food to her grandma like always, but the Big Bad Wolf preys on her. Odysseus wants to get back to his wife Penelope, but the obstacles of the Mediterranean stop him. In Star Wars 4 (SW4), Luke Skywalker wants to find Princess Leia after he receives a message from R2-D2, Obi-Wan insists that he must join the Rebellion, and his foster parents die.

After the setup comes the confrontation: conflict arises when the protagonist faces the obstacle and tries to overcome it. Kana and Lambo elope. Little Red Riding Hood walks through the forest despite her fear of the wolf, who eats her grandma. Odysseus tries to reach home despite the Cyclops, the witch Calypsos, and other seaborne obstacles. Luke tries to save Leia but stumbles upon the

Death Star, Alderaan's destruction, Darth Vader, and the death of Obi-Wan.

Finally, there's the Resolution: the protagonist and the obstacle reach a final clash, and one of them wins. Bok and Lambo fight, but Kana kills her previous partner. The Hunter kills the Wolf, and Grandma and Little Red Riding Hood are saved. Odysseus reaches Ithaca and Penelope eventually recognizes him. Luke Skywalker overcomes Darth Vader's chase and destroys the Death Star.

Some storytelling analysts call the Setup, Confrontation, and Resolution the three acts of a story. But they can look very different in different stories, depending on the story's emotional shape.

The Emotional Shape of Stories

All stories have an emotional shape. Maybe the protagonist lives in a terrible situation that improves throughout the story. Maybe it's the other way around, a tragedy. Maybe he goes through different tribulations, wins, and setbacks.

Kurt Vonnegut proposed in the middle of the 20th Century that there are only a handful of emotional shapes that all stories follow.

Interestingly, his thesis was rejected at the University of Chicago for being "too simple and too much fun"[i]. 35 years later, in 2016, a team of researchers processed 1,700 book stories with machine learning and found that there were in fact 6 types of stories:

1. Rags to Riches: a rise. The Creation Story in Vonnegut's thesis.
2. Tragedy (or Riches to Rags): a fall. From Bad to Worse in Vonnegut's thesis.
3. Man in Hole: fall, then rise.

4. Icarus: rise then fall. Old Testament in Vonnegut's thesis.
5. Cinderella: rise then fall then rise.
6. Oedipus: fall then rise then fall.

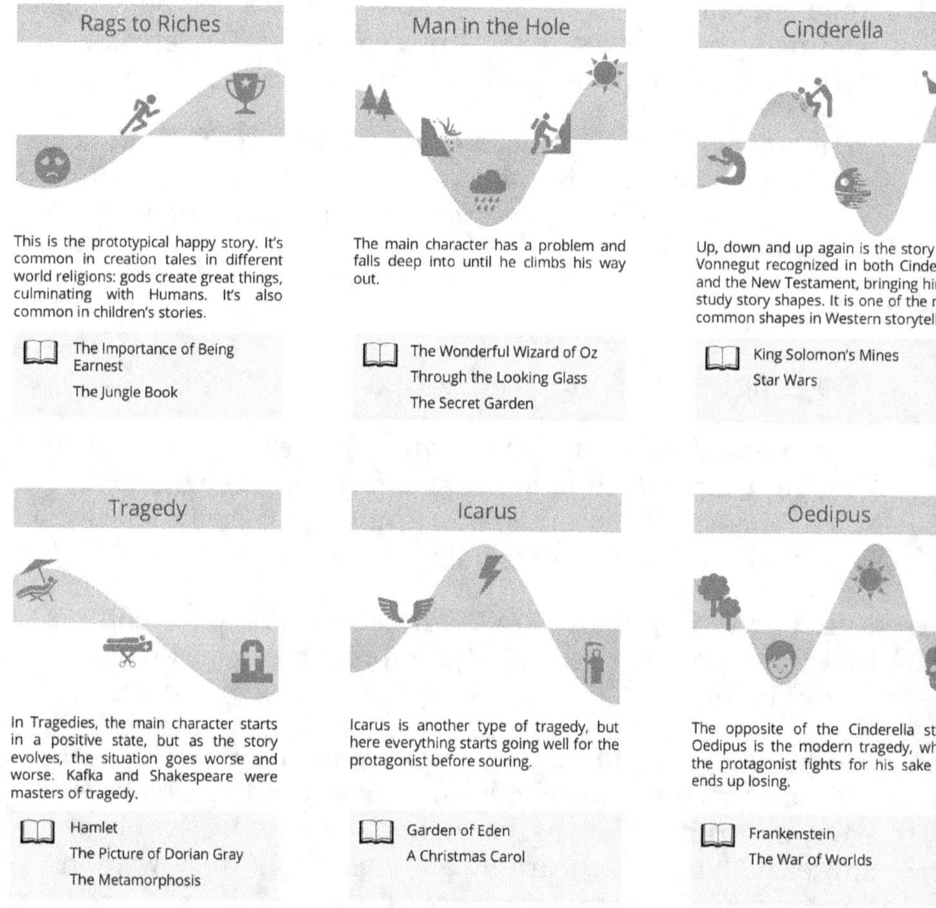

Figure 1 - The six different story shapes according to Artificial Intelligence. Inspired by "The Shape of Stories" from Vonnegut.

Figure 2, below, shows how the Artificial Intelligence (AI) algorithm fit a model story shape to hundreds of different books. The AI, without choosing how many story shapes there would be, ended up with only these 6. The Emotional Shape was assessed by looking at the emotional load of the words used in the books. Words like "happiness" or "laugh" were perceived as very happy, whereas words like "death" or "kill" were very unhappy.

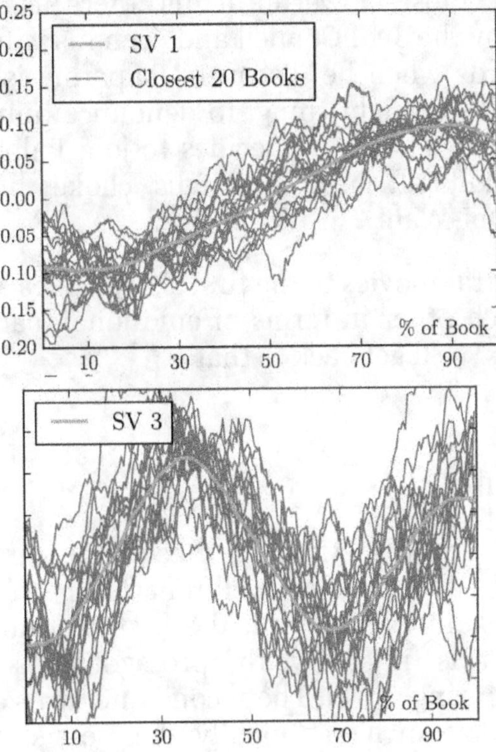

Figure 2 - Two different story shapes uncovered by Artificial Intelligence: Rags to Riches and Cinderella. The grey lines are the 20 closest books to that story arc, and the orange line is the average, paradigmatic story.[ii]

SW4 follows the standard emotional shape of the Cinderella story. Initially, everything goes well: R2-D2 escapes from Darth Vader and Leia resists him; meanwhile, Luke meets Obi-Wan. The story turns around when Leia is questioned, Luke's foster parents are killed, the crew escapes from Stormtroopers, Alderaan is destroyed, and

Obi-Wan dies. Finally, the story ends on a high when Darth Vader is beaten back and the Death Star is destroyed.

Interestingly, while SW4 is the Cinderella story going up, down and then up again, SW3 is the opposite. It's the Oedipus story of a fall, then rise, then fall again. Anakin is one of the most powerful Jedis there is, but he is mistrusted by the Jedi Council and even his wife. The story turns upwards when he discovers Palpatine is a Sith and decides to do the right thing, to denounce him. Finally, it turns back down when he decides to join Palpatine as his apprentice, kills all the young Jedis, chokes his wife, and duels with Obi-Wan.

The two central movies of the first six episodes are a mirror image of each other in terms of emotional load. It's not a coincidence. We'll get back to that.

Act Structure

If the Setup, Confrontation, and Resolution can be seen as three acts, they seem pretty well reflected in the emotional shape of the Cinderella story: the first act starts low and has an upwards trajectory: the protagonist is leaving his normal but boring world. The second one turns around and goes all the way down emotionally: the protagonist is facing the antagonist and things don't go as he wants. The final showdown happens in the third act, reversing the negative trend and ending positively. The same but opposite structure would apply to the Oedipus emotional story shape of going down, up and down again.

But that cut doesn't make sense. It would mean the setup takes more than a third of the story, when most stories have a pretty short setup and leave most of the story for the Confrontation.

So how many acts make up a story? What detailed parts are they made of? You can't believe how many hundreds of writers, beginning with Aristotle over 2,000 years ago, have tried to answer this question, writing about different ways to cut stories into different numbers of acts and beats. Some people swear by 4 acts, other by 5, 7, or 34. Some think there's no structure at all. Below is a list of just 11 authors and 11 opinions. As we can see in Figure 3, however, there are some clear patterns.

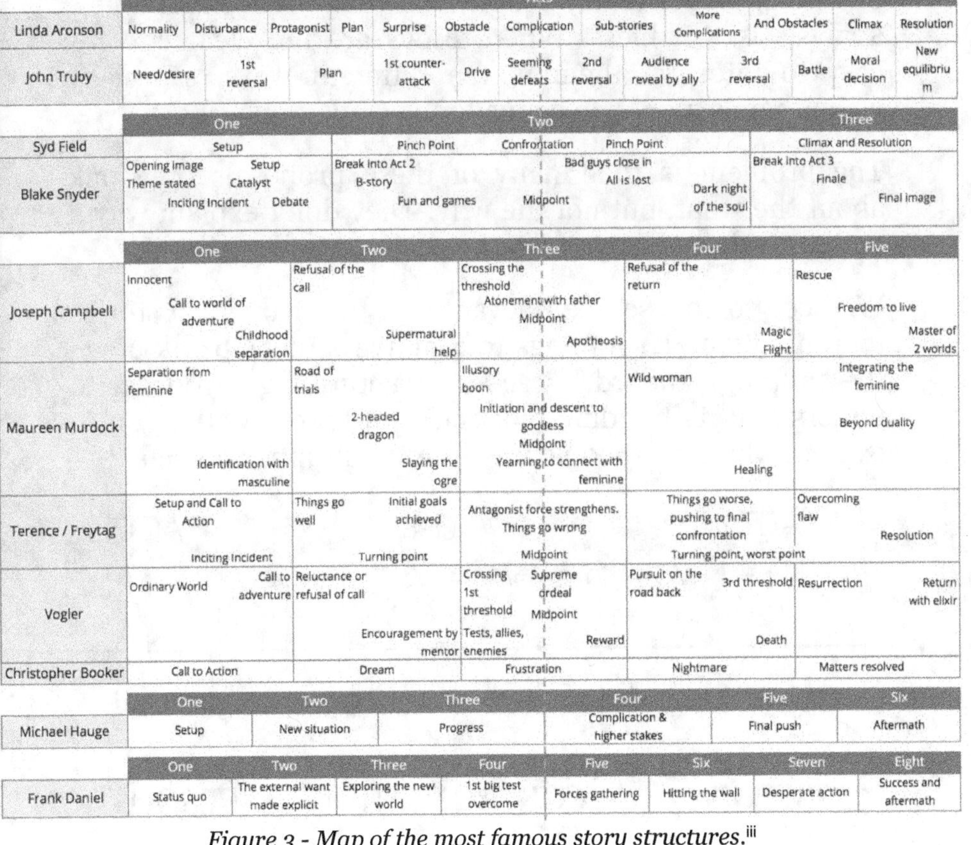

Figure 3 - Map of the most famous story structures.[iii]

It makes sense that there are so many takes on story structures: millions of people's livelihoods depend on storytelling. They want to understand what makes a good story so they can consistently produce more of them. By breaking stories down into pieces, it's easier to see their structure. That's why humans have written about story structure for millennia, and why the market for storytelling structure is always hungry for more.

That's also why many story theorists come up with their own, novel, unique story theory. It sells books to announce a new, unique structure that promises to unlock the magic of stories. And it's pretty safe too: because stories are more psychology than math, nobody can really prove that a new analysis is worthless. When things are not clear cut, it's easy to interpret them in ten different ways, especially when there's money to be made.

The problem is that many of these proposals only talk about the what, but not the why. They don't explain why a structure should be 3, 4, or 34 acts.

We need to choose one relevant way to break down stories to apply its underpinnings to Star Wars. Let's break down the simple, standard, three-act structure first, in order to understand its building blocks. From there, we'll go on to explore why other people use different numbers of acts.

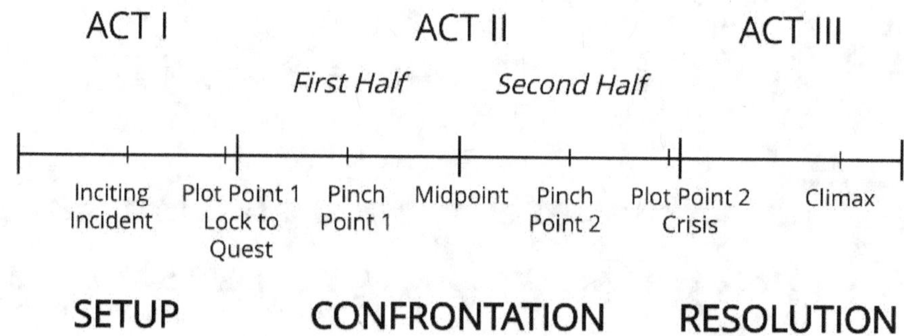

Figure 4 - The Syd Field paradigm of stories.

One of the simplest story structures is the Syd Field paradigm. We'll use 3 famous movies to track this structure: *The Lion King, The Lord of the Rings – The Fellowship of the Ring*, and *Star Wars 4 – A New Hope* (SW4).

The very beginning describes the Status Quo, the world where the protagonist lives. The first event is the Inciting Incident: something that happens to change the Protagonist's Status Quo. After that, the protagonist needs to reflect about the Inciting Incident and decide what to do with it. After pondering what to do, something else happens that pushes the protagonist to embark on the adventure and leave the Ordinary World. It's the Plot Point 1 or Lock to Quest.

The Lion King is the typical story of the boy who becomes a man mixed with *Hamlet*. In the Status Quo, Mufasa and Simba live happily together in the Pridelands. The Inciting Incident has Mufasa tell Simba to avoid the area outside the Pridelands because it's dangerous and he's too young, which irks Simba because he wants to be a grown-up. Scar tells Simba that the secret area is a scary elephant graveyard. Eager to prove he's not a little boy, Simba decides to go there with his friend Nala. This is Plot Point 1.

In *The Lord of the Rings*, the Hobbits are living happily together in Hobbiton when Bilbo disappears in the middle of his birthday speech using the Ring. In Plot Point 1, Gandalf explains the nature of the ring to Frodo and tells him he needs to dispose of it. Frodo decides to leave the Shire to do so.

In SW4, Luke Skywalker is bored but happy on Tatooine. In the Inciting Incident, R2-D2 arrives on Tatooine with a message that Obi-Wan is Princess Leia's only hope. Luke doesn't want to seek Obi-Wan, but R2-D2 leaves on its own to meet him. Luke has no other option: he must leave his Ordinary World of the farm in pursuit of R2-D2, falling into the Extraordinary World of Obi-Wan Kenobi and the Force. This is Plot Point 1.

Plot Point 1 marks the beginning of Act II. You can see it's much bigger than Act I and Act III. In fact, it takes up approximately half the length of the story, as much as Act I and III together. It's split in the middle by the Midpoint. For ease of comprehension, I'll call these Acts 1, 2a, 2b, and 3.

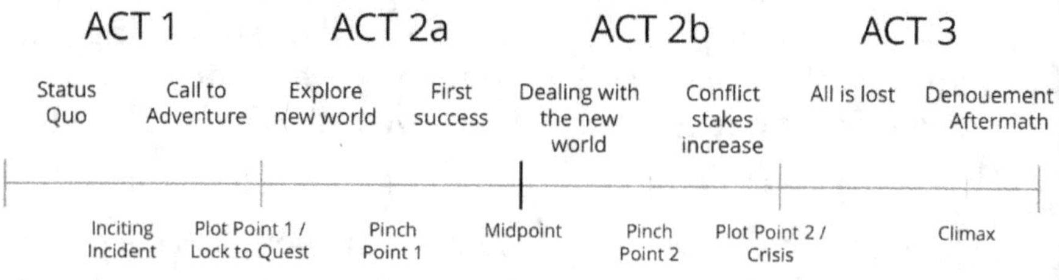

Figure 5

Act 2a explores the protagonist's first steps and successes in this new world. It ends at the Midpoint: an event or revelation that turns the tide of the story and increases the stakes. In the middle, you can see that it has a Pinch: that's the event that will change the direction of the exploration of the new world, increase stakes, and eventually trigger the Midpoint.

In *The Lion King*, Simba's quest is to become a courageous Lion and not just a cub. He leaves the ordinary world of Mufasa's Pridelands and enters the extraordinary world outside the Pridelands. The Pinch 1 is that he and Nala are nearly killed by the hyenas in the Elephant Graveyard. They have a first taste of fear and shame, and feel bad about disobeying Mufasa's ban. That's the pinch point 1.

Scar then uses that to trick Simba into obeying and staying put in the path of a wildebeest stampede. Scar then alerts Mufasa, who, in an attempt to save his cub, ends up dead.

With Mufasa dead, Scar pushes Simba to leave the Pridelands in shame and sadness. This is the Midpoint.

In *The Lord of the Rings*, Frodo and his friends leave the Ordinary World of the Shire to enter the Extraordinary World of the rest of Middle Earth. Pinch 1 is when they're attacked by the black riders and Frodo is stabbed. Rushed to Rivendell, he attends the Council of Elrond, where it becomes clear that only Frodo can take care of the ring. This is the Midpoint.

In SW4, the Pinch Point is when Luke's foster parents are killed. With nothing left in Tatooine, he goes with Obi Wan to Mos Eisley and meets Han Solo and Chewbacca to leave the planet. Meanwhile, Leia resists Darth Vader's questioning to extract the location of the rebels. These events lead to the Midpoint: the destruction of Alderaan by the Death Star, and the Millennium Falcon crew's discovery of the Death Star when they arrive at its location.

Act 2b then repeats a similar structure: first, the protagonist deals with the information from the Midpoint. The second Pinch Point increases the stakes of the story, leading to the lowest point: the end of Act 2b, Plot Point 2. Some call Plot Point 2 the Crisis for obvious reasons: it's a turn that leaves the protagonist in a tough situation for the Resolution.

In *The Lion King*, Pinch Point 2 is when Nala discovers that Simba is exiled, not dead. The Crisis or Plot Point 2 is when Simba decides to come back and confront Scar.

In *The Lord of the Rings*, Pinch Point 2 is when the Fellowship travels through the Mines of Moria and encounters a Balrog. Gandalf fights him to allow the Fellowship to continue their journey. He breaks a bridge, and both he and the Balrog fall. The Fellowship meets with Galadriel in Plot Point 2. Frodo offers her the ring, but she says no and passes the test of resisting the temptation of the ring. Frodo has no alternative but to bring the ring to Mordor to destroy it.

In SW4, in Pinch Point 2 the crew discovers that Leia is held prisoner in the Death Star, so they decide to free her. In the Crisis or Plot Point 2, Obi-Wan Kenobi dies (or disappears) during his lightsaber duel with Darth Vader. The rest of the crew escapes. They now need to plan how to infiltrate the Death Star, because it has followed them to destroy the Rebel base.

That opens the story to Act 3, which will feature a sequence where all seems lost, followed by a Climax and a Denouement. The Climax is the highest suspense: the total confrontation between the Protagonist and Antagonist. The Denouement resolves the Climax.

In *The Lion King*, the Climax is Simba facing Scar. In the Denouement, the betrayed hyenas kill Scar and Simba takes over again.

In *The Lord of the Rings*, the Climax is the attack on the Fellowship of the Ring and Boromir's attempt to steal the ring from Frodo. In the Denouement, Boromir is killed and Frodo escapes with Sam to destroy the ring.

In SW4, the Climax is the attack on the Death Star and the repeated failed attempts to destroy it. The Denouement is when Luke disables the computer and uses the Force to make a one-in-a-million shot to destroy the Death Star.

The story ends with the Aftermath, the state of the world at the end of the story. This is the famed happily-ever-after. It enables the audience to process the resolution and reflect on the changes that happened in the story. Usually, it mirrors the beginning of the story—the status quo—to show the contrast between the main character's original situation and the new one.

In *The Lion King*, the Pridelands are fertile again and Simba and Nala have a new cub, starting a new loop in the

Circle of Life. It's the exact same scene as the beginning of the movie, when Mufasa has Simba. The only contrast is that Simba is now Mufasa, showing his evolution: he has transformed from a cub to a lion, from a boy to a man.

In *The Lord of the Rings*, the Fellowship has split into 2 groups, who will continue their travels together. The contrast is between the indolent, boyish, fraternal life in Hobbiton and the crucial, precarious, distrustful life on the road.

In SW4, Luke and Han Solo are received as heroes and decorated in a ceremony. After traveling all the movie in space confronting the Empire, they're back on a planet free of the Empire. The contrast is between the two initially unreliable, carefree, childish boys into the successful, dependable warriors they've become.

This structure is followed by most stories. Why is that? It seems a bit random. In fact, it's universal. Not because of some esoteric or historical rule, but because its elements are necessary. Let's make sense of them.

You need to start a story by explaining the protagonist and his world. If you don't show the world he comes from, you can't explain why the change matters, or demonstrate a contrast with the end. You also need to share what he likes, his qualities, and his flaws. What he likes is going to define what he eventually wants. The qualities will help him through the journey, while the flaws are what he will need to overcome.

Then, something needs to change that initial situation, the Inciting Incident. Without it, there's no story. It forces the protagonist to change something because his world is not the same anymore. He needs to deal with it, process it, and decide what to do next. It's the Call to Adventure.

From there, he starts exploring the new world. Because he's leaving his status quo, he will meet new characters and be exposed to situations he's never experienced before. He's Exploring the New World.

This exploration will bring him face to face with the forces that changed his world. To make the story more compelling, you want this event to be big, you want it to introduce a new element that raises the stakes of the story, and you want to make sure it taps into the protagonist's flaws to force him to change. This is why the Midpoint is necessary.

At this point, the protagonist needs to cope with this new Midpoint event. It changes what he thought of his Status Quo and New World, his wants, and his flaws. That's why the next phase needs to be Dealing with the New World.

As he deals with that new world, he will take some actions that change the story and lead to Pinch Point 2. He's now pushing hard against the obstacle he's fighting. Doing so will lead to an increase in the stakes of the conflict: the obstacle is not easily defeated.

This leads to the Crisis, a moment where the stakes between the protagonist and the antagonist reach their maximum intensity. This point necessarily lays all the elements on the table in a way that is compelling and high-stakes, and makes it clear what choice needs to happen during the Resolution.

Now all the pieces are laid out. The protagonist is in a dire situation and is preparing to finally deal with the obstacle. This confrontation happens in the Climax. It's the moment of maximum opposition. The Denouement resolves the Climax's conflict.

After that, the audience needs to learn the lesson of the story and cope emotionally with what just happened. This is the Aftermath.

Let's put all of this together for SW4. What does its Act structure look like? It meticulously abides by this structure to a surprising level. Indeed, George Lucas is famous for following narrative structure very closely. The movie is exactly 120 minutes long, with 4 acts of precisely 30 minutes each, split every time into two pieces of 15 minutes each. Every event happens extremely close to these 15 minute marks.

You can see in Figure 7 that Lucas's story structure was extremely disciplined. He did not deviate from it at all. It's not just that the story follows each beat literally. Every beat happens within a few minutes of where it should theoretically happen. For example, the midpoint happens in minute 62 instead of minute 60. Obi-Wan disappears in minute 92 instead of minute 90. Time and again, Lucas has demonstrated his devotion to proper story structure.

This already gives us a hint about the entire saga: George Lucas is obsessed with story structure and follows it quite literally. He had a blueprint, and he was going to use it in his movies. You can assume many things about him, but you can't assume he doesn't meticulously follow story structure.

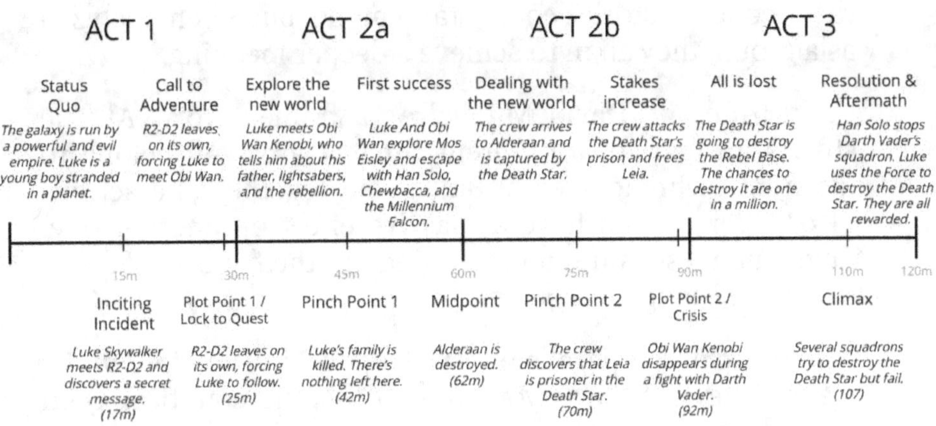

Figure 6 - The 3-act structure in Star Wars Episode IV – "A New Hope".

Framed, Parallel and Nested Structures

The structures discussed so far only consider the main story. In reality, every book and movie has different sub-stories intertwined, and all follow a similar pattern.

For example, in SW4, aside from the movie itself, we have Luke's story, evolving from a boy into a man with the Force. R2-D2 and C-3PO have a love-hate relationship. Han Solo is so stressed by his debts that he can only think of monetary rewards, until, in the end, his friends become important enough that he risks his own life for them. Leia is a senator for Alderaan who has to make a choice between her planet and the rebellion. She cunningly avoids making a choice, but loses her planet regardless.

Secondary stories can be framed, parallel, or nested. Framed stories are different stories that build up to a major one. Parallel stories will use at least two very different—but closely related—stories, which occur at around the same time and make up one main story. Nested stories will have several smaller stories inside a larger one. In all of these, the secondary stories could stand alone, but when analyzed as a group, they align to achieve a deeper meaning.

Cloud Atlas by David Mitchell is a framed story. All the stories are part of a different time or area. All belong to different technology eras. But, taken together, the actions of one person can have a massive effect on another one. Love, madness and understanding are the fruits of life and can often change its course.

An example of a parallel story structure is *The Holiday* by Nancy Meyers. Two women in different counties, both struggling to find happiness, trade homes and undergo a journey of personal growth. Their paths reconnect, portraying the ways they both find fulfillment in life.

Inception, written and directed by Christopher Nolan, is nested both inside and outside the movie. The characters nest themselves into deeper and deeper stories in the mind of the host, but the deeper stories need to be resolved before the first ones can be resolved.

In SW4, saving Leia is a story nested inside the broader story of the Death Star's threat against the Rebellion. The relationship between R2-D2 and C-3PO is transactional at the beginning, but they become friends over the course of the movie. This story runs parallel to Han Solo's, who has a very transactional relationship with the rest of the crew at the beginning, which he eventually transcends when he becomes friends with Luke and Leia.

Darth Vader's story runs parallel to Luke's, although the parallel only becomes obvious in the next movie, SW5. In SW4, he's just an almighty antagonist. But if we consider SW4 through SW6, we see the parallel stories much more clearly. For Luke, the evolution is to go from a weak boy to a Jedi in SW4, to be tempted by the Dark Side in SW5, and to finally choose the Light Side in SW6. Meanwhile, Darth Vader is a powerful Sith of the Dark Side in SW4, he's tempted to join the Light Side by the existence of his son in SW5, and he finally turns to the Light Side in SW6.

So, between SW4 and SW6, Luke and Darth Vader have parallel stories that span three movies, with nested stories for each movie. We can see that George Lucas's obsession with narrative structure extends beyond a single movie.

Circular Stories

So far, we've examined stories that follow a clear line from the beginning to the end. Linear narrative is the most common and basic type of story. A linear narrative has a clear beginning, middle, and end, and they appear in a linear sequence.

However, stories don't need to be linear. In fact, many follow a circular shape. We've already discussed how many stories have an Aftermath similar to the Status Quo to demonstrate contrast. Some movies do this more than others. For example, *The Lion King* has an ending that's exactly the same as the beginning, with the lion king presenting his baby cub to the savanna, except that Simba replaces Mufasa. Even the song is called the Circle of Life! Conversely, *The Lord of the Rings* contrasts the beginning and the ending with very different settings. Frodo does not return to Hobbiton changed. He's alone, with only Sam for a companion, embarking on a very different mission and lifestyle. He does return to Hobbiton at the end of the book series, changed after the epic journey to Mordor.

We've covered how SW4 is somewhat circular, but its circularity becomes more obvious when we use the Hero's Journey, a very well-known type of circular story.

The Hero's Journey

The Hero's Journey is another breakthrough in understanding storytelling, developed in the middle of the 20th Century. Joseph Campbell, a mythologist, compared the stories in all religions and belief systems and found similar patterns. It looked as if all stories were just one: the Hero's Journey.

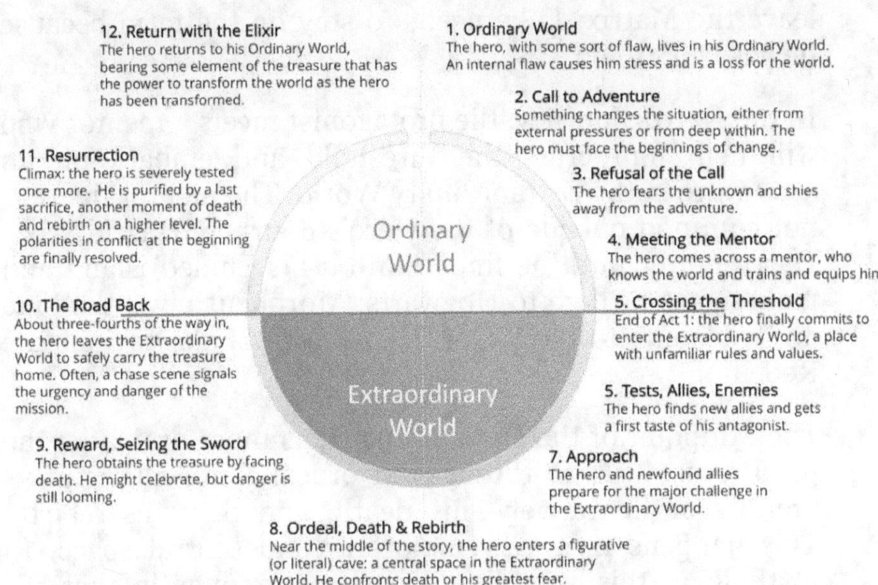

Figure 7 - The structure of the Hero's Journey, from Joseph Campbell's "Hero with a Thousand Faces".

The Hero's Journey is similar to what we've already seen, but with a few crucial nuances.

The hero's Status Quo is an Ordinary World, and the New World is an Extraordinary World in contrast. A normal book or movie might have the entire plot happen in one single context, but in the Hero's Journey there's a clear Ordinary World, and when the protagonist leaves for his quest, he enters a truly Extraordinary World: Hogwarts for Harry Potter, outside the Matrix for Neo, space for Luke...

In the Hero's Journey, the hero initially refuses the call, which is not the case for most stories. It's important because the Hero's Journey is about a normal person who has to step up to become a hero. Hence, he needs to initially refuse the call to clearly mark the fear of engaging. Harry Potter doesn't initially accept that he's a wizard in the first book; Neo doesn't take on the first invitation to leave the Matrix; Luke needs to stay on the farm because he has work to do.

In the Hero's Journey, the protagonist meets a mentor who will help him cross the threshold and embark on an adventure in the Extraordinary World. The mentor figure is not common outside of the Hero's Journey. Hagrid seeks Harry Potter until he finds him on a secluded island and makes sure he'll go to Hogwarts; Morpheus gives the blue and red pills to Neo; Obi Wan pushes Luke to join the Rebellion.

The Midpoint of the Hero's Journey is more dramatic: the protagonist will go through an ordeal that will signify—literally or figuratively—his death, and then his rebirth. This happens in a very important and central space. In mythology, this is a literal cave so frequently that it's referred to as "The Cave". Harry Potter enters a dark place guarded by a dangerous three-headed dog and discovers the truth about the Sorcerer's Stone. Neo goes to the Matrix to see the Oracle, who tells him he is not the Chosen One and reveals he will have to choose between Morpheus's life and his own. Luke finds Alderaan destroyed and is captured by the terrible Death Star.

After confronting this experience, the hero will obtain a reward, with which he goes back to the Ordinary World. It's the knowledge of the stone in Harry Potter; the special power to bend the Matrix for Neo; the Force and the plans to the Death Star for Luke.

George Lucas was the first to identify the potential of the Hero's Journey for a movie. He read the theory while working on the script for Star Wars, and was shocked to recognize similar patterns. He decided to rewrite Star Wars to make it fit the Hero's Journey more closely.

12. Return with the Elixir
Luke and the rest of the crew are back from the Empire's threat, with the discovery of the Force.

1. Ordinary World
A poor boy lives with his broken family in a desert planet. He has great skills handling robots, and a special gift as a pilot.

2. Call to Adventure
A representative of the extraordinary world (R2-D2) arrives with a mission (find Obi Wan).

11. Resurrection
Luke is still a normal boy trying to hit the Death Star but misses, until he kills the normal boy in him and embraces the Force, resurrecting as a Jedi and destroying the Death Star

3. Refusal of the Call
Luke doesn't want to find Obi Wan. He has other things to do.

4. Meeting the Mentor
R2-D2 leaves. Luke is forced to follow him. He meets Obi Wan.

Ordinary World

10. The Road Back
The crew lands in friendly territory, the Rebel Base, and starts planning how to attack the Death Star.

5. Crossing the Threshold
Luke's family is killed. Nothing left, he leaves for the Extraordinary World.

6. Tests, Allies, Enemies
Luke leaves his world and goes to Mos Eisley, where he meets his new allies Han Solo, Chewbacca and their Millennium Falcon.

Extraordinary World

9. Reward, Seizing the Sword
The crew escapes with Leia, who unlocks the plans of the Death Star that include its weak spot. This crucial information will enable the Rebellion to attack the Death Star.

7. Approach
The crew narrowly escapes the Stormtroopers and the Empire, jumping into hyperdrive.

8. Ordeal, Death & Rebirth
When they arrive, Alderaan is destroyed and they are captured by the Death Star, the deadliest weapon in the galaxy. They nearly die trying to free Leia and in the garbage compactor. Obi-Wan dies, and revives through the Force, talking to Luke.

Figure 8 - The structure of the Hero's Journey applied to Star Wars Episode IV – "A New Hope".

It is very clear that George Lucas also followed the blueprint of the Hero's Journey for SW4. A clear picture of George Lucas is emerging, of a man following storytelling structures with zeal.

The Midpoint and Symmetry

Most people tend to focus on the Climax and Resolution as the most important part of a story, but if you look at the map of story structures shared previously, you'll see that the Midpoint appears nearly everywhere and is strongly highlighted. Why?

It's because the key revelation of the story takes place at the Midpoint. The Midpoint unveils the key truth that the protagonist was missing in his Ordinary World, and that he needs to accept before he can solve the problem that led him to the Extraordinary World. It exposes his flaw, the lie he's been telling himself, the thing he needs to change.

For the first half of the story, the protagonist is leaving his old world and exploring the new one. This exploration culminates at the midpoint. In the second half of the story, the protagonist will deal with this revelation until he's back to the initial point, changed.

The midpoint is the mirror of a story. The peak of a mountain. Everything that happens in the first half will be mirrored in the second.

In SW5 – The Empire Strikes Back, the midpoint is when Luke Skywalker goes into a literal cave, has a vision of Darth Vader, faces his fear of him, and sees himself in the helmet of Darth Vader. This is the midpoint of SW5: before that, Luke was growing arrogant in his blind trust of the Light Side. At this midpoint, he realizes he also suffers his father's flaw: he has the Dark Side in him too. This is also the Midpoint of the entire trilogy of SW4-6, which is not a coincidence, as we'll see later.

SW4 follows the Hero's Journey as a circular story, but it also follows a mirror image of itself.

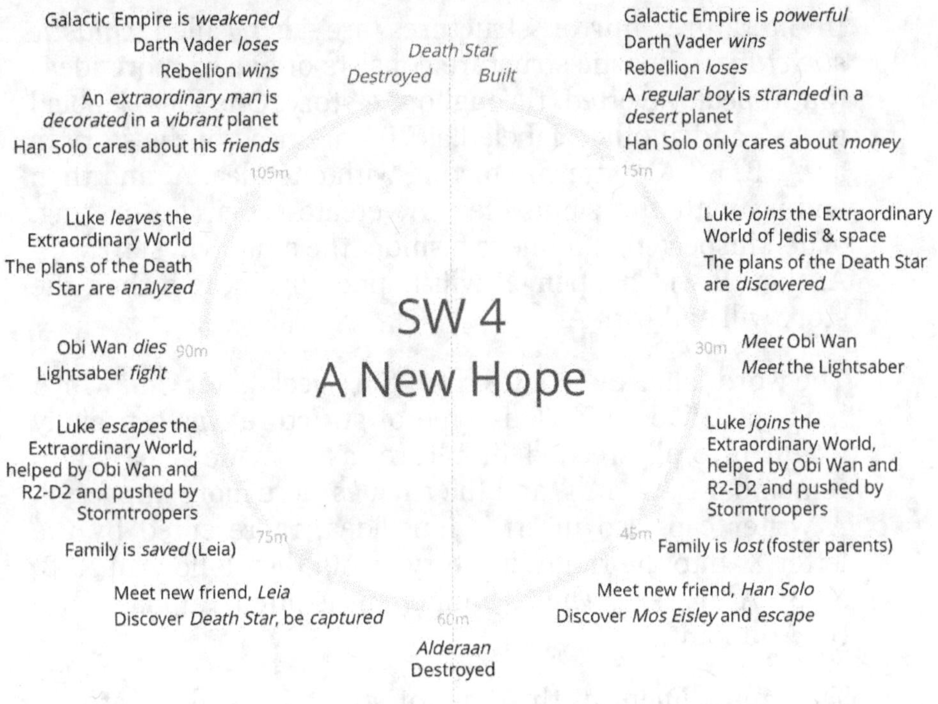

Galactic Empire is *weakened*
Darth Vader *loses*
Rebellion *wins*
An *extraordinary man* is *decorated* in a *vibrant* planet
Han Solo cares about his *friends*

Death Star
Destroyed — *Built*

Galactic Empire is *powerful*
Darth Vader *wins*
Rebellion *loses*
A *regular boy* is *stranded* in a *desert* planet
Han Solo only cares about *money*

105m — 15m

Luke *leaves* the Extraordinary World
The plans of the Death Star are *analyzed*

Luke *joins* the Extraordinary World of Jedis & space
The plans of the Death Star are *discovered*

SW 4
A New Hope

Obi Wan *dies*
Lightsaber *fight*
90m

30m
Meet Obi Wan
Meet the Lightsaber

Luke *escapes* the Extraordinary World, helped by Obi Wan and R2-D2 and pushed by Stormtroopers
Family is *saved* (Leia)

Luke *joins* the Extraordinary World, helped by Obi Wan and R2-D2 and pushed by Stormtroopers
Family is *lost* (foster parents)

75m — 45m

Meet new friend, *Leia*
Discover *Death Star*, be *captured*

Meet new friend, *Han Solo*
Discover *Mos Eisley* and *escape*

60m

Alderaan
Destroyed

Figure 9 – Mirror structure of Star Wars Episode IV – "A New Hope"

You can see in Figure 9 that every beat of the story is reflected in the mirror side of the movie. For example, the movie starts with a powerful Galactic Empire, a win for Darth Vader, and a loss for the Rebellion; it ends with the Galactic Empire weakened by a loss for Darth Vader and a win for the Rebellion. Or you can see that around minute 30 (25% into the movie), Luke meets Obi-Wan and his lightsaber, and in minute 90 Obi-Wan dies in a lightsaber duel. This was the first time George Lucas used perfectly-mirrored stories, but as you can imagine it was not the last...

Chiastic structure

In literature, mirror structures are also called *chiastic structures*. Chiastic structure consists of two or more ideas that repeat, inverted, throughout a story. One idea, labeled as "A", and another, labeled as "B", are used in the story in an A, B, B', A' pattern. Starting with one idea, A, and then ending with the same idea, A, creates a circle, or ring. When inspected in a linear fashion, the story will start with A, then B will happen, B will happen again, and then the story will end with A.

The word "chiastic" comes from the Greek letter Chi, which looks just like an X. This type of structure was especially useful in orally-recited literature, as it made it easier to remember the words, and the rhymes were more impactful. A writer can also insert a lone idea, represented by the letter X, into the ring. The story would then follow an A, B, X, B', A' pattern. The X component is often emphasized – the Midpoint.

The embodiment of this type of structure is like that of a mirror. The components in these types of stories reflect each other in the forms of words, ideas, themes, personal storylines, images, events, colors, and so on.

There are some common sayings that are simple forms of chiasma; for instance, the saying "When the going gets tough, the tough get going" is chiastic. Another saying refers to the chances of finding a mate in life with the following chiasma: "Around these parts, the odds are pretty good, but the goods are pretty odd". Notice how the "odds" and "goods" or the "going" and "tough" are interchanged to convey a certain idea. Sure, you could say things like, "Well, when times are tough and you find yourself struggling, strong people pull themselves up and face it head on" or things like, "Around here, the chances of finding a single, available mate are pretty good, because there are a lot of them; however, most of these single available people have strange personality quirks or are a bit eccentric". The ideas portrayed are the same, but chiastic sayings drive the idea home and make it truly memorable. Which would you rather remember? Ben Franklin's famous axiom "By failing to prepare, you are preparing to fail"? Or its bare idea, laid out in the form of "If you are not preparing for the coming hardship, you may end up in a sticky situation where your life or the lives that depend on you are put at risk"? I think we can all agree that the former is more appealing.

Fractals

The last story element we need to introduce is the Fractal. But what is a fractal?

Figure 10 - Image of a fractal: the same patterns are replicated again and again across different orders of magnitude.

A fractal is an image that repeats itself regardless of the scale at which you view it. If you zoom in or out a lot, you still see a similar shape.

Stories can be fractal, too. Fractal stories don't just have one big arc. Instead, they are made up of many smaller arcs that follow the same structure. We've talked about the three-act structure. The same logic is valid for every act, even every scene. A situation, a conflict, an exploration of the conflict, a midpoint, an exploration of the midpoint, and a climax and resolution exist within each act, within each scene, within each sequence.

For example, what are the Pinch Points? They are the Inciting Incidents of Acts 2a and 2b. The Midpoint is just the Climax of Act 2a. Plot Points 1 and 2 are the Climax of Acts 1 and 2b respectively.

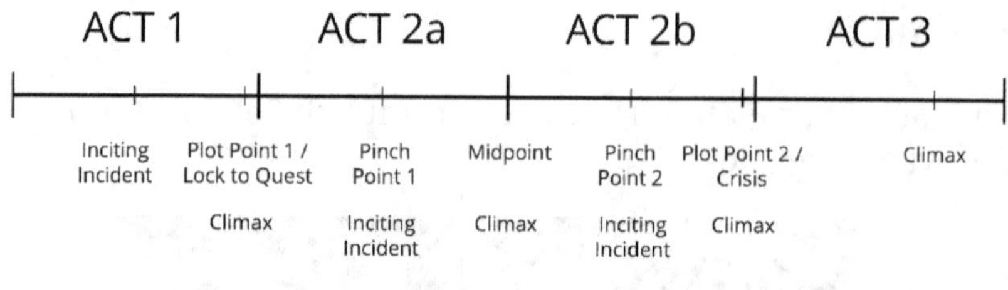

Figure 11

If you look at the emotional structure of Harry Potter 7 – *Harry Potter and the Deathly Hallows*, you can see many things emerge.

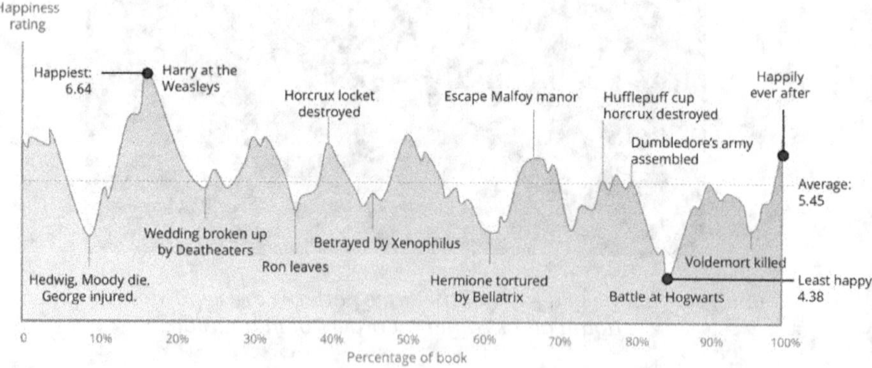

Figure 12- The story of Harry Potter 7 – Deathly Hallows follows a series of ups and downs for each sub-story. Overall, however, it follows the Cinderella story of Up, Down, Up.

First, this has a broad Cinderella story shape, with the story going up to the happiest point with Harry Potter at the Weasleys'. Then it goes down, all the way to the Battle at Hogwarts, before going up again.

The Inciting Incident and the Crisis can be deduced too. The first trough, with Harry Potter's escape and the death of Hedwig and Moody, happens just after the Inciting Incident. The Crisis is the lowest point of the story, and sure enough, the least happy moment is at the end, with the Battle of Hogwarts.

But the overall story shape is made up of lots of ups and downs. If we were to zoom into these ups and downs, we would probably see smaller ups and downs. Each one of them follows its own standard narrative structure.

The emergence of story structures at different levels is what is called the fractal nature of a story. Like mathematical or real-life fractals, the same structure repeats itself at the micro level, the macro level, and all the levels in between.

Many good stories have a fractal structure within a given movie or book. But what happens when storytellers become really ambitious with the fractal properties of their story? They create Rings.

Chapter 2: Ring Theory

Few stories in history have had enough ambition to take the fractal nature of storytelling to new levels by using repeating patterns not only across verses, pages, chapters, or volumes, but across full epics. These stories are called Rings.

A Ring might have, for example, a movie that is circular for the main character, but also for secondary characters. Minor scenes within that movie could be circular. Then, the movie could have a sequel that is circular both on its own and as part of a bigger story with the first movie. For example, the end of the first movie can be the Midpoint of the combination. The end of the second movie is an aftermath that mirrors the status quo of the first one, and so on.

Figure 13 - Conceptual illustration of a Story's Ring Structure.

A very good, recent example of ring structure is Harry Potter, as indicated recently by John Granger. Spoiler alert: I'm going to discuss all the books and movies at length.

Harry Potter

In the first book of the series, Harry Potter starts as a young boy in the ordinary, non-magical "muggle" world. He receives a Call to Adventure: the news that he is a wizard and needs to go to Hogwarts for training.

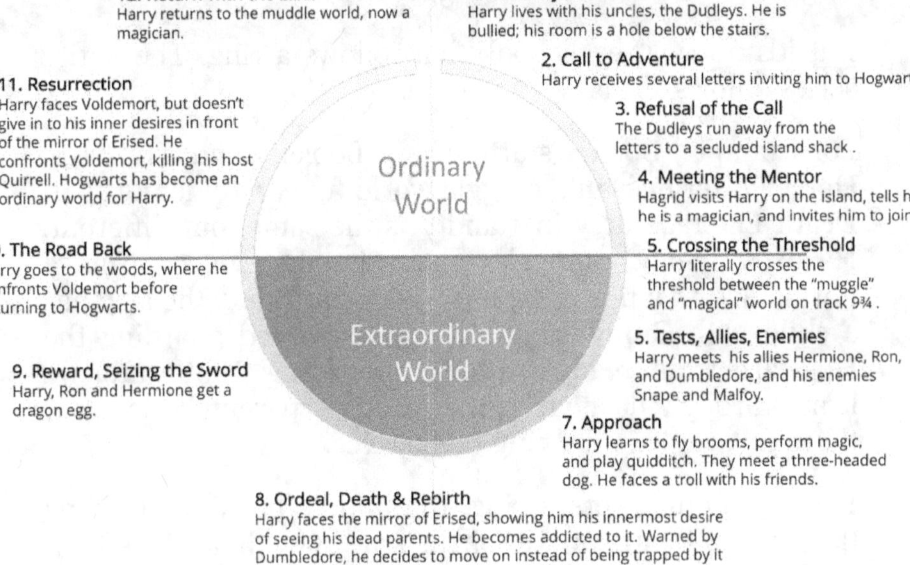

Figure 14 - The Hero's Journey for "Harry Potter and the Sorcerer's Stone" (first book and movie).

It's not just the first book that follows this structure. Each book in the series has a very similar structure: Harry begins and ends the year in the same Ordinary World of normal people, or "muggles". He enters the Extraordinary World of Hogwarts, where he faces an Ordeal. Close to the end, he confronts Voldemort and the Death Eaters in one way or another. At the end of each book, he goes back to the Ordinary World. Each one of the books follows the same Hero's Journey, which is also mirrored or chiastic. This ambition transcends a standard story structure. It has a Ring structure, each movie being one of the rings.

Inside the books, there are also specific rings. For example, when leaving the "Ordinary World of Hogwarts" and going to the "Extraordinary World" of Hogsmeade, the village outside of Hogwarts that is not as protected by magic. Or leaving Hogwarts for the forest. There's also the train ride, the Quidditch games, the winter break, the points tally at the end of the year... Every year is a book or movie, and every year these smaller patterns are repeated like small rings that contribute to the bigger ring.

But it's not just each book that follows a ring. The entire series follows a ring.

For example, Book 1 starts where Books 7 ends. In both, Harry Potter lives in a muggle world free of Voldemort and Death Eaters. Harry in 1 and 7 is the same, but different. He lives amongst muggles again, but he evolved from a normal kid to a powerful and wise wizard. In 7, he also has a child with Ginny. That child is presented boarding the Hogwarts train, ready to start another ring. That's after we learn through flashbacks that Harry's parents also went through a very similar ring themselves.

If Harry Potter were a ring, the middle book would have the Ordeal, Death, and Rebirth. True enough, at the end of Book 4 of 7, Harry meets the true Voldemort for the first time in his embodied shape, and a friend dies. Harry witnesses death for the first time. The middle book of the series is the middle book of the ring.

J.K. Rowling points out some of the rings herself in an interview for the extras on one of the movies. She says there is a "link" between Lily (Harry Potter's mother) and

Narcissa (Draco Malfoy's mother). Lily sacrifices herself for Harry and pays with her life. In the end of the last movie, Narcissa saves Harry by lying to the dark leader, Voldemort, because of her son Draco. Harry didn't kill Draco, and Narcissa is grateful. Rowling points out that a mother's sacrificial love trumps all, even in the midst of evil.

She also touches on how she couldn't kill off Hagrid (the Hogwarts gamekeeper and Harry's friend) because he had to be there to carry Harry out of the forest after Voldemort thought he killed him in their last duel. Hagrid also carried Harry as a baby after Voldemort killed his parents, and he carried Harry out of the Ordinary World in the first book. Hagrid's ring is there to carry Harry through his darkest of times.

She also hints that she had to kill off Professor Lupin. He was married to Nymphadora Tonks, and they had a son named Teddy. Lupin was one of Harry's great mentors; he taught him a great deal about himself. Rowling said she had to kill Lupin because it would make an orphan out of Teddy in the same way that Harry was left an orphan.

Rings are everywhere in Harry Potter.

<u>Blood Sacrifice and Protection</u>

Book 1: Harry finds out that his mother, Lily, sacrificed herself to protect him from Voldemort, thus erecting a blood protection.

Book 4: Voldemort realizes he cannot touch Harry while the protection spell is still there, so he uses Harry's blood to be reborn into the world, thus breaking the spell and doubly connecting himself to Harry.

Book 7: The blood connection between Harry and Voldemort ends up keeping Harry alive longer when he and Voldemort have one of their last duels.

<u>Ollivander's only parts in the books</u>

Book 1: When Harry is shopping for his first year at Hogwarts, he is sent to get a wand. Ollivander's shop is the place to go, where we hear the iconic line from Ollivander, "The wand chooses the wizard".

Book 4: Ollivander inspects Harry's wand and is told to take better care of it.

Book 7: After being kidnapped, imprisoned, and tortured, Harry Potter rescues Ollivander and takes him to a safe house. Harry questions him about wand lore, the connection between his wand and Voldemort's, and wand loyalty. At the end of the movie, Harry breaks a wand.

<u>The only times Dragons are present and the ties from innocence to a world-weary Harry</u>

Book 1: Norbert is a baby dragon that Hagrid foolishly tries to keep and tame. Harry finds out about it, and then Malfoy does. They all get detention, and the baby dragon is sent away.

Book 4: Harry is enrolled in the Triwizard Tournament, and one of the tasks requires him to steal a mother dragon's egg. The egg is actually the clue to the next task, but the dragon still thinks it's hers.

Book 7: The last book features an old, blind, decrepit, and chained dragon that is locked away in a bank to protect high-end vaults. Harry and his friends must get past the dragon; they end up freeing the dragon and fleeing with it.

Dragons appear in the first, middle, and last book as a baby, mother and elder. They represent the passage of time, the stages of life, and the aging of Harry.

Some other parallels between books 1, 4 and 7:

- Harry only sees his parents through magical items, in Book 1 with a magical mirror, in Book 4 with a spell, and in Book 7 with a magical stone.
- Harry rides on Sirius's motorcycle with Hagrid in the beginning, going to the Dursleys' house, and leaving it in the seventh book.
- In Harry's first game of Quidditch, he almost swallows the Golden Snitch. In the end, when his mouth touches the Snitch, it opens for him revealing something he needs.
- In the first book, on Christmas night, Ron sees his deepest desires in a magical mirror. In the last book, also on Christmas night, Ron sees his deepest fears in a magical locket.

Obviously, the mirror image is not just valid for books 1, 4 and 7. Books 2 and 3 mirror books 5 and 6. For example, we meet Sirius Black in Book 3, and we say goodbye to him in Book 5.

Harry Potter is just the most recent and successful application of ring structure. Before J. K. Rowling, George Lucas was the first mainstream moviemaker to apply a ring structure to his works, thanks to Joseph Campbell's discoveries about the Hero's Journey. That, in turn, came from analyzing mythological stories from around the world, such as the Bible, the Koran, or the well-known Anglo-Saxon epic, Beowulf.

Since they were the inspiration for Joseph Campbell's breakthrough in storytelling structure, let's have a look at the structure of old mythologies and religious books.

Beowulf

Beowulf is one of the most ancient Old English tales that has survived to modern times. It was one of the inspirations for the Hero's Journey. In fact, it adheres to a full-on ring structure. For example, you can see here the mirror image (or chiastic structure) of the Introduction and Conclusion.

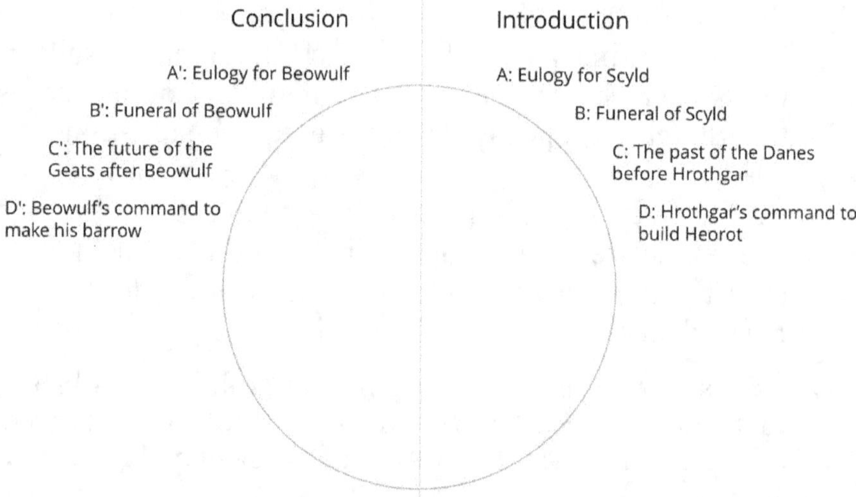

Figure 15 - Beowulf's chiastic structure in the introduction vs. conclusion.

The chiastic structure of the Introduction and Conclusion are obvious. The rest of the story is made up of three main battles. Each of the battles follows a chiastic structure too. For example:

A: Grendel approaches, rejoices, and eats Handscio.
B: Grendel wants to run after his fingers are cracked.
C: The Danes are terrified and scream in the hall.
X: Heorot is in danger.
C': The Danes are terrified and scream in the hall.
B': Grendel is forced to flee; his joints break, his arm is torn.
A': Aftermath: Grendel runs away while Beowulf rejoices with Grendel's arm.

Each one of the three stories themselves represent a ring:

1. Beowulf faces Grendel and kills him, becoming famous. It's the beginning of his story.

2. Beowulf faces Grendel's mother and kills her, becoming legendary. It's his apotheosis.
3. Beowulf faces the dragon and kills it, but dies in the process. It's his twilight.

Furthermore, in the last battle, Wiglaf is the only warrior to help Beowulf kill the dragon. He is like Beowulf a generation earlier. The beginning of a new Ring

It's pretty incredible that a story that's over a thousand years old follows such a sophisticated ring structure. Let's think about this for a moment: most writers today still don't master a story structure that was already in use *a thousand years ago*.

It is probable that authors of stories like Beowulf drew inspiration from some of the most important books in history, the religious ones. For example, the Bible, probably the most published and read book of all time, is filled with rings.

The Bible

While the Bible has always been analyzed for its authenticity, literary composition, and storylines, its ring structure is not so widely discussed. For example, the flood in Genesis is an elaborate chiasm:

A: Start with Noah and his sons (Genesis 6:10)
B: Every life on the Earth (Genesis 6:13)
C: The curse on the Earth (Genesis 6:13)
D: The Flood is announced (Genesis 6:7)
E: The Ark (Genesis 6:14–16)

F: All God's creatures (Genesis 6:17–20)
G: Our food (Genesis 6:21)
H: The animals are in man's hands (Genesis 7:2–3)
I: Boarding the Ark (Genesis 7:13–16)
J: The water rises (Genesis 7:17–20)
X: God and Noah (Genesis 8:1)
J': The water dries up (Genesis 8:13–14)
I': Leaving the Ark (Genesis 8:15–19)
H': The animals (Genesis 9:2–3)
G': Our food (Genesis 9:3–4)
F': All God's creatures (Genesis 9:10)
E': The Ark (Genesis 9:10)
D': No flood will happen in the future (Genesis 9:11)
C': God's blessing on the Earth (Genesis 9:12–17)
B': Every life on earth (Genesis 9:16)
A': End with Noah and his sons (Genesis 9:18–19)

Following a proper ring structure, the numbers 40, 7, and 150 also follow a chiasm:

A: 7 days until they can enter the Ark (Genesis 7:4)
B: Another mention of 7 days to wait (Genesis 7:10)
C: 40 days (Genesis 7:17)
D: 150 days (Genesis 7:24)
X: God and Noah (Genesis 8:1)
D': 150 days (Genesis 8:3)
C': 40 days (Genesis 8:6)
B': 7 days they wait for a dove (Genesis 8:10)
A': Another 7 days they wait for a dove (Genesis 8:12)

Same thing for the book of Proverbs:

A: Proverbs 1:20–21. Wisdom calls and there is a cry out.
B: Proverbs 1:22. Those who are foolish hate knowledge, and how long will simple people love their simplicity? Because those who scorn others, love it.
C: Proverbs 1:23. I will pour my spirit on to you, I will make my words known. Turn away from my rebuke.

D: Proverbs 1:24–25. I called to you but you refused me. You disdained all my advice and had none of my rebuke.

E: Proverbs 1:26–28. I will laugh at your calamity, mock you when terror finds you, when it comes in and destroys you, they will call to me but I will not answer. They will seek me but will not find me.

D′: Proverbs 1:29–30. Because they hate knowledge and do not chose to fear the Lord, they won't have any of my advice and will despise my every rebuke.

C′: Proverbs 1:31. Therefore, they will do as they wish and be filled with their own desires.

B′: Proverbs 1:32. The simple and the fools will be destroyed by their own complacency.

A′: Proverbs 1:33. But if you listen to me, you will be safe and secure, not fearing evil.

Chiasmas can be found even in the phrasing of sentences. In Jesus's own words in Mark 2:27, "The Sabbath was made for man, not man for the Sabbath". In simple A, B, B′, A′ form, the words Sabbath and man are used and then repeated in reverse order. The same format is used in Matthew 23:12, "For those who exalt themselves will be humbled, and those who humbled themselves will be exalted". In this case, exalted and humbled play the roles of A and B.

The Koran

The Koran's passages, themes, and words are also cycled through in rings. For example, this verse, from the Sūra 91 (The Sun), opens with a divine oath that is complex, made up of a series of parallelisms:

"وَالشَّمْسِ وَضُحَاهَا: By the sun and its brightness
وَالْقَمَرِ إِذَا تَلَاهَا: By the moon when it follows it,

وَالنَّهَارِ إِذَا جَلَّاهَا: By the day when it displays it,

يَغْشَاهَا إِذَا وَاللَّيْلِ: By the night when it veils it,

بَنَاهَا وَمَا وَالسَّمَاءِ: By sky and the One who built it,

طَحَاهَا وَمَا وَالْأَرْضِ: By the earth and the One who spread it..."

Another example in 6:95:

الْحَيِّ مِنَ الْمَيِّتِ وَمُخْرِجُ الْمَيِّتِ مِنَ الْحَيِّ يُخْرِجُ

A(A): He brings the living out
B (B): from the dead
B′ (A'): and brings the dead out
A′ (B'): from the living.

This is a perfect example of an advanced chiasma at the lowest level: words. There is an ABB'A' chiasma when looking at the concepts of living and dead, but grammatically there is an ABA'B' structure. This repeat-and-mirror structure at all levels of a story is the most salient evidence of a ring structure.

The Book of Mormon

It isn't only the older, widely-followed religious books that use a ring structure. The Book of Mormon also has a ring structure:

A: "as surely as the Lord liveth" (3 Nephi 5:24)
B: "gather in from the four quarters of the earth" (3 Nephi 5:24)
C: "restoring all the house of Jacob unto the knowledge of the covenant" (3 Nephi 5:25)
C′: "then shall they know their Redeemer, who is Jesus Christ" (3 Nephi 5:26)
B′: "gathered in from the four quarters of the earth unto their own land" (3 Nephi 5:26)
A′: "as the Lord liveth" (3 Nephi 5:26)

Another chiastic passage is in Alma 36 – The Conversion of Alma

A: "inasmuch as ye shall keep the commandments of God ye shall prosper in the land" (Alma 36:1)
B: "remembering the captivity of our fathers" (Alma 36:2)
C: "whosoever shall put their trust in God shall be supported in their trials" (Alma 36:3)
D: "I racked, even with the pains of a damned soul (Alma 36:12) I remembered...the coming of one Jesus Christ, a Son of God, to atone for the sins of the world" (Alma 36:17)
D': "O Jesus, thou Son of God, have mercy on me (Alma 36:19) I could remember my pains no more" (Alma 36:19)
C': "I have been supported under trials" (Alma 36:27)
B': "delivered them out of bondage and captivity" (Alma 36:29)
A': "inasmuch as ye shall keep the commandments of God ye shall prosper in the land" (Alma 36:30)

The Ring Structure

Clearly, fractals and chiastic structures are a cornerstone of storytelling and writing in old religious and mythological books. They unearthed a human truth that other authors have recycled since. We've touched on the concept of a ring structure, and covered a few famous works that follow one. It's time to formally describe it: what is a ring structure?

A story that follows a Ring Structure is usually a Hero's Journey with a chiastic shape that includes several other smaller chiastic stories and components. The similarities between components are represented by key events or key words. There is often a thematic link between one section and its chiastic counterpart, because they share the same—or antithetical—components.

Putting it all together, there are at least eight rules you can use to recognize—and build—a Ring Structure:

1. A Hero's Journey: the story will follow the structure of a Hero's Journey, extracted from an Ordinary World into an Extraordinary World by a mentor despite his reluctance, facing an ordeal with a rebirth, leaving with a special power to the Ordinary World, facing the Antagonistic forces one last time, and dying and resurrecting as a Hero with the Elixir.

2. The exposition: We're presented with the status quo of the main character theme. What his world is like, what he wants, and his flaws. Then, an inciting incident changes that world. It's a dilemma that must be addressed, a doubt that must be satisfied. It sets up the midpoint as the point where a key insight is learned, and where the key flaw is faced.

3. Central loading: the middle point is very important and key events happen there that change the course of the first half. It's the moment when a key insight is learned, a key milestone reached, or a key protagonist flaw exposed.

4. Two halves: The ring must split into two halves at the midpoint. The event is so impactful that the story starts turning back. The first half involved exploration, while the second half returns to the original situation to deal with the midpoint revelation.

5. Sections that are parallel: The two halves that separate at the midpoint must be parallel. This is achieved by making the components that oppose each other across the dividing line—from the beginning to the midpoint— similar in some respect. For example, in a buddy story, the first half will feature events that bond two characters, while the second half will feature similar events that separate them instead.

6. Individual components are tagged by indicators: The individual components of the story within the ring structure must be marked in some way, such that the

person viewing the material will know where and when each section starts and stops.

7. Rings within rings: A larger ring will make up the entire story, while many smaller rings may be present within the same story. Some rings will span the entire length of the main ring. Others will be shorter, or nested. They will all mirror each other in terms of characters, settings, themes, morals, and so on. They can also come from different authors, times, or sources. Some stories will also be composed of many tiny rings, which will make incorporating older material easy, relatable, memorable, and interesting.

8. Closure of all rings times two: Lastly, the ending of the main ring has to join up with the beginning and make a precise closure on both the thematic and structural levels. The beginning will have been designed to accept the ending and coincide with it. When the ending comes into reach, the viewer will recognize it, and will expect to see the similar events or themes they saw in the beginning. Every ring must follow that blueprint.

A story that employs the ring structure is not meant to be seen in a linear fashion. To examine a ring structure story linearly would be to misinterpret it. Instead, the best way to view it would be circularly. This means that each segment on the ring is important and adds its own bit of information to tell the whole story. The full meaning of the whole story can only be grasped when compared in every direction instead of just one. Stories that may have seemed confusing to unprepared readers turn out to be expertly controlled and complex when read through the right lens.

This is what happened with the most famous Ring Structure of all times, Star Wars.

PART II – THE RINGS OF STAR WARS

Chapter 3: Rings in the Star Wars Movies 4–6

When *Star Wars 1 – The Phantom Menace* arrived in theaters in 1999 after more than a decade of waiting, expectations were high. They soon turned to distress when the audience saw a movie that seemed so similar to the original trilogy, yet with new patterns that didn't make sense to them, accompanied by what was seen as bad writing, directing, and acting.

When SW7 – *The Force Awakens* – was released in 2015 after yet again more than a decade of waiting, people feared that the same thing would happen with the new sequels. But fans loved it. Yet, again, they complained that it was eerily similar to SW4 – *A New Hope*. Why was it so similar? Why did people like it so much if it wasn't that novel? And why do all the movies have this sense of repetition?

According to Anne Lancashire, a professor of Cinema Studies and Drama at the University of Toronto, repeating the story patterns throughout the saga gives it "a sense of repeating, increasingly complex cycles of human experience", through individual lives, and across generations[iv]. The variations emphasize an ever-repeating but ever-changing history. The broad pattern of human life, from youth to maturity to death, remains constant, but individual circumstances within the pattern incvitably differ, creating different possibilities and problems". Obviously, this is not just human at the personal level, but at the social and political levels too, with the rise and fall of democracies and dictatorships.

George Lucas has also talked about repetition in his saga, usually with a music allegory. According to him, Star Wars "is purposely written like a piece of music, with themes that repeat themselves in different ways, and ideas that reprise from one generation to the next"[v]. For example, when comparing Luke with Anakin, he says: "Instead of destroying the Death Star, [Anakin] destroys the ship that controls the robots. It's like poetry. Every stanza kind of rhymes with the last one"[vi].

Mike Klimo has extensively documented how George Lucas has used Rings to structure Star Wars[vii], especially regarding the cinematographic parallels between movies. Whether Lucas already thought in terms of rings for the original trilogy or not, he actually built it following a ring structure.

The Ring of Star Wars 5 – The Empire Strikes Back

We've already covered how SW4 is a Hero's Journey and is also chiastic. But it's not the only movie to follow a ring structure in Star Wars. Every movie of the original trilogy follows one. Let's look at the chiastic structure of SW5.

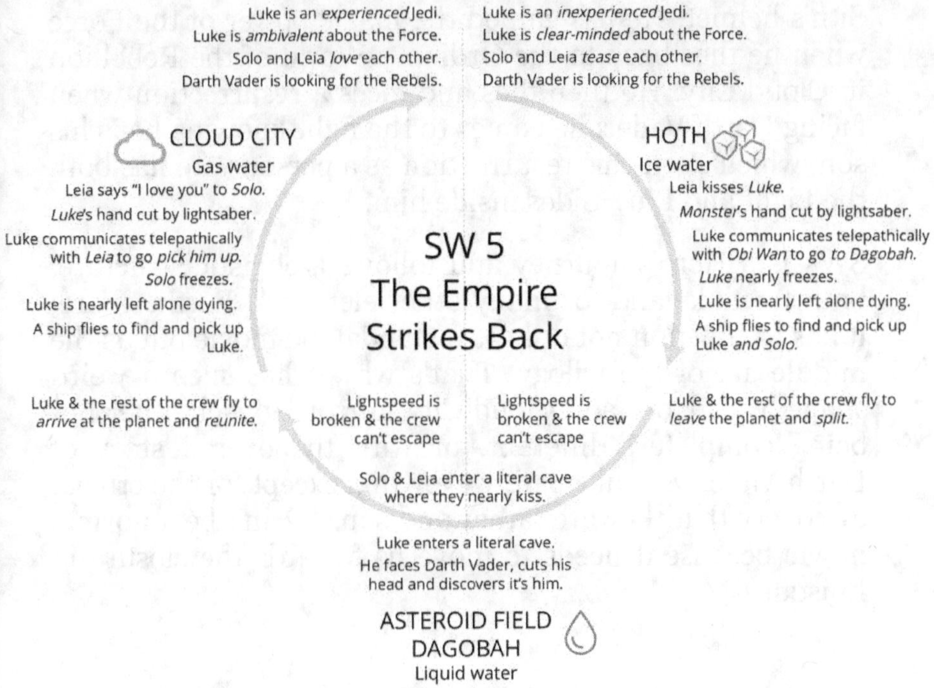

Luke is an *experienced* Jedi.
Luke is *ambivalent* about the Force.
Solo and Leia *love* each other.
Darth Vader is looking for the Rebels.

Luke is an *inexperienced* Jedi.
Luke is *clear-minded* about the Force.
Solo and Leia *tease* each other.
Darth Vader is looking for the Rebels.

CLOUD CITY
Gas water

Leia says "I love you" to *Solo*.
Luke's hand cut by lightsaber.
Luke communicates telepathically with *Leia* to go *pick him up*.
Solo freezes.
Luke is nearly left alone dying.
A ship flies to find and pick up Luke.

HOTH
Ice water

Leia kisses *Luke*.
Monster's hand cut by lightsaber.
Luke communicates telepathically with *Obi Wan* to go *to Dagobah*.
Luke nearly freezes.
Luke is nearly left alone dying.
A ship flies to find and pick up Luke *and Solo*.

SW 5
The Empire
Strikes Back

Luke & the rest of the crew fly to *arrive* at the planet and *reunite*.

Lightspeed is broken & the crew can't escape.

Lightspeed is broken & the crew can't escape.

Luke & the rest of the crew fly to *leave* the planet and *split*.

Solo & Leia enter a literal cave where they nearly kiss.

Luke enters a literal cave.
He faces Darth Vader, cuts his head and discovers it's him.

ASTEROID FIELD
DAGOBAH
Liquid water

Figure 16 - Chiastic structure of Star Wars 5 – "The Empire Strikes Back".

The chiastic structure of SW5 is obvious. It's divided in 3 precise thirds. The first third, Hoth, mirrors the last one, Cloud City, in every respect. For example, on Hoth, Leia kisses Luke and Luke cuts a monster's limb off with a lightsaber, whereas in Cloud City Leia says "I love you" to Han Solo and Luke loses his limb because of a lightsaber. The middle third shows two stories in parallel that mirror each other. Luke goes to Dagobah and enters a cave. At the very same time, Leia and Han Solo are in another cave in an asteroid field.

The Hero's Journey is also obvious. Luke leaves the Ordinary World of the Rebellion to go train as a Jedi on Dagobah. He meets his Mentor, who wants to teach him the ways of the Force, but Luke is too pretentious and arrogant for that. He enters a literal cave, where he faces the Ordeal of Darth Vader and sees his own face in the

Sith's helmet. He has gained the magic power of the Force when he flies back to the Ordinary World of the Rebellion in Cloud City. He then dies and faces a resurrection when facing Darth Vader: he comes to the fight knowing he is his son, which opens his resurrection as a person who has both the Light and Dark Sides inside him.

SW5 is a Hero's Journey and follows a chiastic structure, both for Luke and for many other elements. Furthermore, it has to function not only as a standalone movie but as the middle act of the trilogy. That's why it has such a weird shape, with Hoth and Cloud City mirroring each other but being completely different, or with the overall story of Darth Vader vs. Luke barely evolving, except for the crucial discovery that they are father and son. It can't be a normal movie because it needs to move us towards the closure in Episode 6[1].

Luke's Ring in SW4–6

It also means that the Midpoint of SW5 is the Midpoint of the entire trilogy.

In SW4, Luke discovers the Force and beats the Dark Side with the Force. In SW5, Luke is with Yoda in Dagobah and enters a very literal cave – reminiscent of the Hero's Journey figurative cave. There, he faces Darth Vader, cuts his head, and discovers his own head in the helmet. That is the Hero's Journey's Ordeal, Death and Rebirth, showing Luke that the Dark Side is part of him too. It's the Midpoint of the series, from Light Side to Dark Side.

At the end of the movie, when Darth Vader tells him that he is Luke's father, that acts as the Denouement of SW5,

---

[1] SW6 in fact also follows a chiastic structure with a Hero's Journey, but since it's the exact same concept, I'll leave it to you to pick the movie apart.

but also as the Pinch Point of the entire trilogy. How will Luke react in the final act with this revelation?

Finally, SW6 functions mainly as the trilogy's Act 3. Luke will have to decide between the Light Side and the Dark Side of the Force. At the last moment, he decides not to kill the Emperor, thus closing not just the ring of SW6, but the ring of the entire trilogy.

The Ring of the Dark Side in SW4–6

Darth Vader follows the same ring, but mirrored. Instead of starting out weak with the Force and becoming strong on the Light side, he turns to the Dark Side first.

In SW4, he begins strong with the Dark Side of the Force. At the end of SW4, he notes that the Force is strong with Luke. That is the Inciting Incident of the arcs of both Luke and Anakin.

Over the course of SW5, he discovers that Luke is his son. That sheds doubts on his belief in the Dark Side. It's the midpoint of his turn to the light side. In SW6, he turns to the Light Side and dies, weak. He has returned to his original state.

The Empire follows the exact same structure as Darth Vader's. It starts strong, dissolving the Senate and destroying Alderaan. As the movies advance, it becomes more and more unstable, losing the Death Star once, then attacking the Rebels without much success, and losing the Death Star again. At the end, with the Emperor's death, it starts unraveling. The Rebellion mirrors that evolution: the Empire's failure is the Rebellion's success.

SW4 and 6 also echo each other with a similar storyline. In both cases, the Death Star is about to annihilate the Rebel Base, but, at the last minute, the Rebels manage to destroy the Death Star.

The Full Ring of the Original Trilogy

There are several rings to follow across the original trilogy: the rings of Luke, Darth Vader, Han Solo, Leia, the Jedi Mentors, the Death Star, the Empire vs. the Rebellion, and the Light Side vs. the Dark Side. If we put them all together, this is what it looks like.

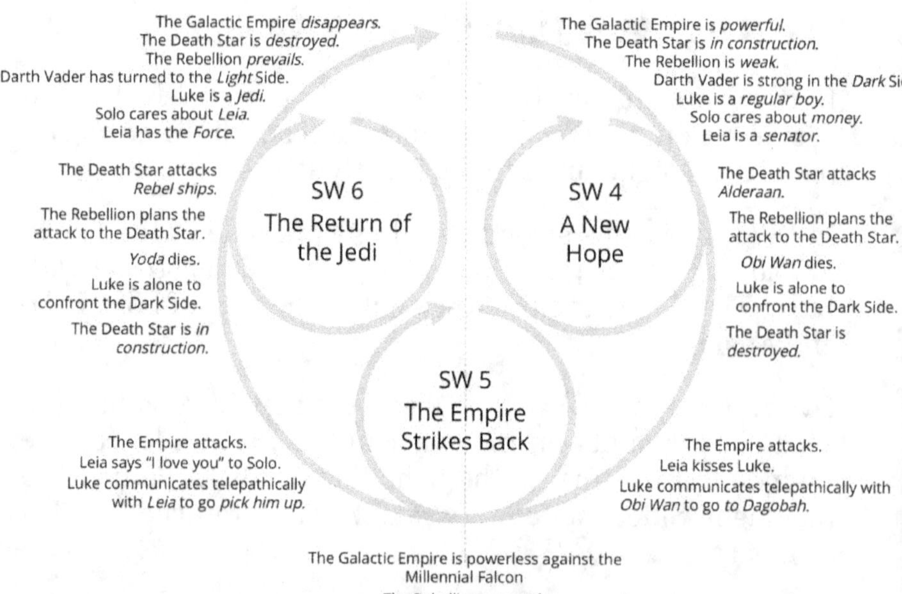

Figure 17 - Chiastic structure of Star Wars 4 through 6.

Not only did George Lucas create SW4, SW5 and SW6 as chiastic structures with a Hero's Journey for each. The entire trilogy is chiastic. It also follows a Hero's Journey for Luke and Han Solo, and the mirror image of that journey for Darth Vader.

Chapter 4: Rings across the First Six Movies

George Lucas's ambition in creating the original Star Wars was staggering. He built a Ring Epic not only inside each movie, but also across the entire original trilogy.

Not content with that, he decided to expand the ring structure with the prequel trilogy, creating an immense Ring through the first 6 episodes.

Many of these rings are very similar to the ones we've already seen in the original trilogy. In this chapter, we will examine these rings. They will range from character rings, politics and themes to the balance of light and dark forces. Let's start with the most obvious and beloved one.

The Ring of the Protagonists

Anyone who has ever watched these movies noticed the similarity between Luke and his father Anakin (also known as Darth Vader). Both boys start out life as poor, good-hearted, and innocent. They are both from the barren planet of Tatooine, with nothing but sand and desert. The planet is run by the Hutts, with the slimy, giant worm Jabba as its leader. Anakin lives in a broken family: a slave, with a mother and no father. Luke also lives in a broken family: an orphan, working on a moisture farm with his Uncle and Aunt. Both boys have uncanny skills building droids, flying, and using the Force.

In both cases, a pair of friends discovers them. C-3PO and R2-D2 discover Luke, and Qui-Gon Jinn and Obi-Wan discover Anakin. Both discover Obi-Wan early on, and both eventually become his padawan. Both lose their master in the first movie: Qui-Gon for Anakin and Obi-Wan for Luke.

Luke learns of his destiny to become a Jedi through Obi-Wan Kenobi and leaves the planet with him, thus beginning his journey. Luke destroys the first Death Star in Episode 4 by firing two shots into an exhaust vent, stopping the Empire and winning the battle. Then, after the death of his first mentor, he is taught the ways of the force by Yoda. After his training, Luke encounters his nemesis, Darth Vader. He loses his right hand in a battle with him but escapes to fight another day.

Similarly, Anakin learns of his destiny to become a Jedi from Qui-Gon Jinn and leaves Tatooine with him, thus beginning his journey. Anakin unintentionally destroys the command ship that is controlling the droid army in Episode 1 by firing two shots at the main reactor, incapacitating the army and winning the battle. After his first mentor dies, he is taught the ways of the force by Obi-Wan Kenobi. During his training, he falls in love with Senator Amidala and marries her in secret. Anakin loses his right hand in a battle with a powerful Count Dooku, but lives to fight another day.

Luke is seduced by the Dark Side when he learns that Darth Vader is a parent, his father. At the end of his trilogy, when another beloved one is threatened – his sister Leia – he overcomes fear. The Emperor pushes him to choose the Dark Side by killing a third person – Darth Vader – but he chooses the Light Side and stops fighting.

Anakin is seduced by the Dark Side when he loses a parent, his mother. At the end of his trilogy, when another beloved one is threatened (Padmé) he falls to fear. The Emperor pushes him to choose the Dark Side by killing a third person (Mace Windu) but he chooses the Dark Side, which triggers a rampage. At the end of the movie, he duels Obi-Wan on the planet Mustafar, where he loses all his limbs and completes his transformation into Darth Vader. "Mustafa", by the way, means "Chosen One" in Arabic.

The protagonist's arc can be explained in a simple thread.

Episode 1: Anakin is recruited to begin training as a Jedi.
Episode 2: Anakin trains as a Jedi and is tempted by the Dark Side.
Episode 3: When Anakin must choose between the Light Side and the Dark Side, he chooses the Dark Side.
Episode 4: Luke is recruited to become a Jedi and fight with the Rebels; Anakin is strong with the Dark Side.
Episode 5: Luke trains as a Jedi and is tempted by the Dark Side; Anakin is tempted by his son to join the Light Side.
Episode 6: When Luke must choose between the Light Side and the Dark Side, he renounces the choice; when Anakin must choose between the Light Side and Dark Side, he chooses the Light side.

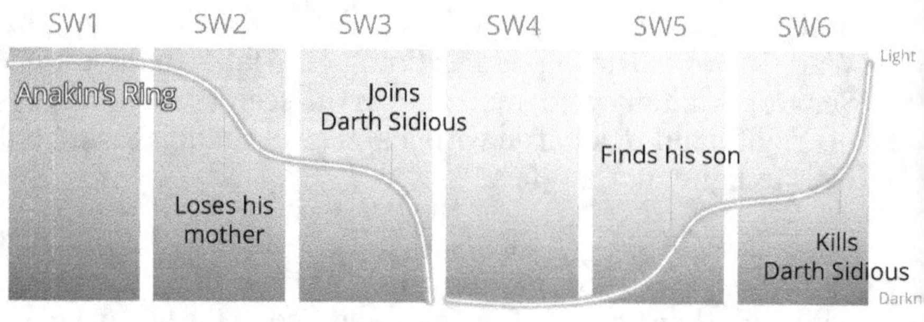

Figure 18 - Anakin's Ring in SW 1-6.

If we map the evolution of Anakin over movies 1 through 6, this is what we see.

The mirror image of Anakin's arc in SW1-3 and SW4-6 is obvious when the trilogies are stacked.

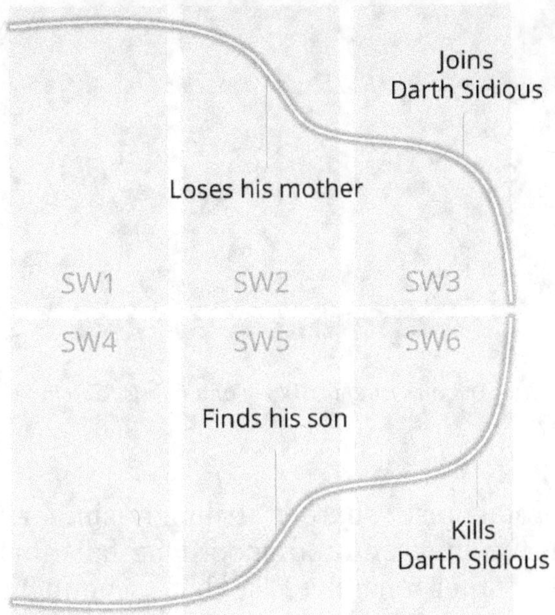

Figure 19 - Anakin's Ring in SW 1-6, stacked.

If we add Luke's Ring, this is what the six movies look like:

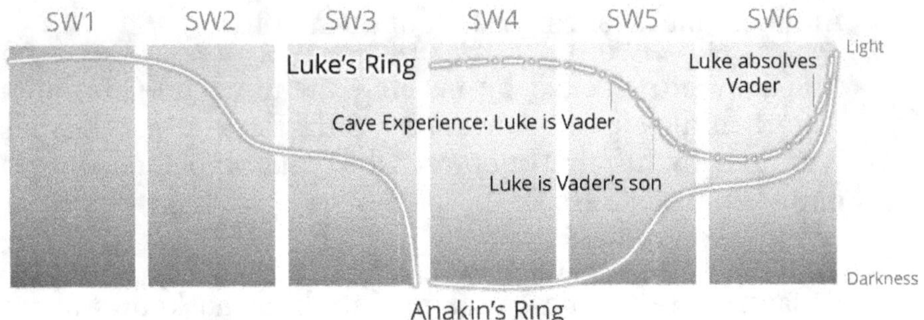

Figure 20 - Anakin's and Luke's Rings in SW 1-6.

Overlapping the trilogies highlights the parallels and mirror images of both rings.

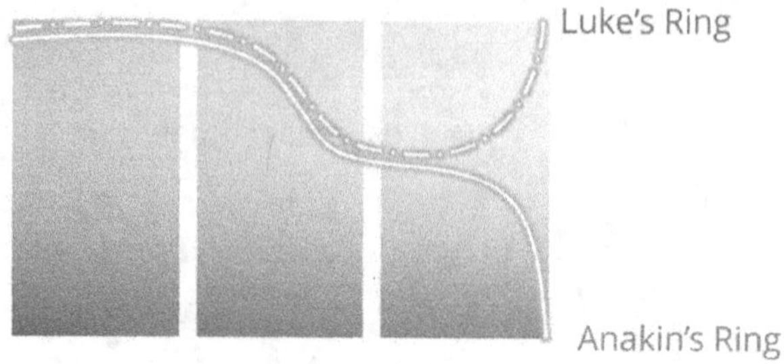

Figure 21 - Anakin's Ring in SW 1-3 and Luke's Ring in SW 3-6.

The two protagonists share a strikingly similar arc. They both begin life innocent and good. One falls for the Dark Side, and the other renounces the fight, seemingly choosing the Light. Since Anakin's arc is to fall and then rise, this begs the question: how will Luke's arc pan out?

The Mentor's Ring

Another character ring is that of the mentor.

Anakin was recruited by his first mentor, Qui-Gon Jinn, who then dies in battle against a Sith, Darth Maul. Luke is recruited by his first mentor, Obi-Wan, who then dies in battle against a Sith, Darth Vader,

Anakin is then taken under the wing of Obi-Wan as his padawan. He teaches Anakin everything he knows about the Force, but Anakin is young and impulsive and wants to become a Jedi before he's ready. Luke is taken under the wing of Yoda as his padawan. He teaches Luke many ways of the Force, but Luke is young and impulsive and leaves to help his friends before he's ready.

Luke faces his father in the last fight of SW6, and his father ends up dying. For Anakin, Obi-Wan is a fatherly figure: in Episode 2, Obi-Wan and Anakin are walking into a bar when Obi-Wan jokingly says, "Why do I get the feeling you're going to be the death of me?" To which Anakin replies, "Don't say that, Master, you're the closest thing I have to a father." At the end of SW3, Anakin faces his fatherly figure, Obi-Wan. Obi-Wan doesn't die there, but ends up dying in SW4.

The mentor's arc can be explained in a simple thread;

Episode 1: Anakin's first mentor dies.
Episode 2: Anakin learns from his second mentor.
Episode 3: Anakin opposes his mentor and fatherly figure, who ends up dying
Episode 4: Luke's first mentor dies.
Episode 5: Luke learns from his second mentor.
Episode 6: Luke opposes his fatherly figure, who ends up dying.

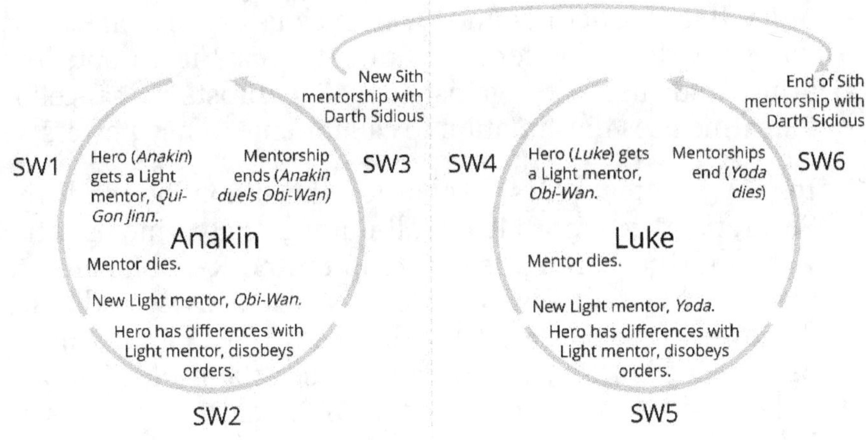

Figure 22 - Mentorship Rings in Star Wars 1 through 6.

The Political Ring

The original trilogy skirted the topic a bit, but the prequel trilogy was bathed in politics. It is the story of the Republic destroyed and replaced by the Empire, which is then also destroyed and replaced by a New Republic and First Order.

In SW1, we are brought into the inner workings of the senate on the planet Coruscant. The Republic is in control of the galaxy but has reached a standstill with the Trade Federation regarding the planet Naboo. Since her planet is being blocked from trading, Queen Amidala seeks a speedy resolution in the senate. Unable to achieve that, she presents a vote of no confidence against the existing chancellor. Palpatine, senator for Naboo, takes advantage of this power vacuum and the goodwill towards Naboo to become Chancellor.

In SW2, a Separatist movement emerges that aims to secede from the Republic and attack it. Anakin discovers the plot. Meanwhile, Obi-Wan finds out that a clone army is ready for use by the Republic. Allegedly, an old Jedi had ordered it. The Jedi Council is suspicious of the clone army, but with the imminent Separatist threat, it co-opts the army and uses it against the Separatists. Chancellor Palpatine uses the situation to call for emergency powers.

In SW3, after years of battle, the Republic and the Separatists are embroiled in all-out war. Palpatine uses the war to further strengthen his grip on the Republic and its Senate. In a moment of weakness, when most Jedis are deployed in warzones, Palpatine uses the Clone Army to betray and kill them. He then accuses them of a coup to tighten his grip on the Senate. The Senate acquiesces to Palpatine's declaration amidst a celebratory ovation. Padmé captures the moment with what is probably the most famous quote of the prequels: "So this is how liberty dies, with thunderous applause."

In the original trilogy, though it's not front and center, the politics arc progresses in the background. At the beginning of SW4, the Empire has a strong grip on the Senate, but it still needs a delicate balance to prevent new separatist movements. That's why it builds the Death Star and destroys Alderaan: no planet would dare to challenge the Empire with such a weapon. This is the pinnacle of the Empire's power. Only a small rebel force contests its unrestrained power. Luke joins the Rebels and destroys the Empire's new weapon.

With the growing Rebel fleet in SW5, the Empire strikes back against the Rebels, but they don't capture anything of value. Even a tiny ship like the Millennium Falcon wreaks havoc in the Empire's fleet by dragging it into an asteroid field.

In SW6, the Empire is not almighty anymore. It is in the midst of the construction of the second Death Star, but it's exposed. It's reduced to laying a trap for the Rebels to catch them. When the Rebels destroy its shield, their upgraded fleet easily destroys the new Death Star. At the end of the movie, the demise of the Empire is celebrated across the galaxy.

The politics arc can be explained in a simple thread.

Episode 1: The Republic is functional, with very few threats.
Episode 2: The Republic launches a preemptive strike against a growing threat.
Episode 3: The Republic falls, replaced by the rising Empire.
Episode 4: The Empire is functional, with very few threats.
Episode 5: The Empire launches a preemptive strike against a growing threat.
Episode 6: The Empire falls, replaced by the rising Rebels and First Order.

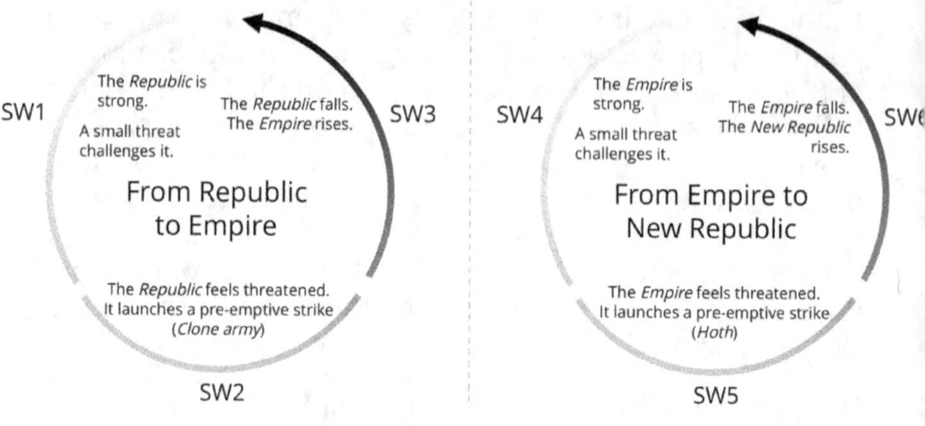

Figure 23 - Political Rings in Star Wars 1 through 6.

The Theme Ring

The main theme of this series is the struggle between Light and Darkness, the eternal human conflict between Good and Evil. Should we do the right thing or succumb to temptation? Should we put others first, or should we be selfish? Should we use power for our own benefit, or should we put it at the service of others? Should we follow our instincts, or should we override them with rational thought?

The fight between Light and Darkness pervades religions. It is best represented by the Yin and Yang, the eternal conflict between Light and Darkness that together form a whole.

Figure 24 – Yin and Yang symbol.

Through the first six movies, Star Wars explores the theme of good vs. evil by following the rings of Politics and Anakin.

In SW1, we see the Republic as a weak source of stability. The Light Side of the Force is strong, nurtured by an established Jedi Council and numerous Jedis policing the Galaxy. Threats are scarce. Darkness only peeks in through Darth Maul and Darth Sidious's handling of the Trade Federation and its droids. Anakin is good-natured.

SW2 shows a grown-up Anakin. He is still good, but some of his personality traits and decisions start to look worrisome. The Dark Side grows in numbers and creates a force to be reckoned with, in the form of the Separatist movement led by Count Dooku. Darkness openly challenges Light. Fear and danger are looming in the Galaxy, and an uneasy feeling persists, leading the viewer to believe that something terrible is going to happen in the next installment.

SW3 delivers the ending we dreaded as we see the fall of Anakin, the extinction of love, the annihilation of Jedis, the ruin of the Republic, the disintegration of the old order, and the triumph of evil.

In SW4, pure evil rules the galaxy. Darth Vader is strong on the Dark Side, the Emperor has unchecked power, and the Empire becomes the destroyer of worlds. A hint of Light emerges though Luke's innocence and goodwill. The destruction of the Death Star offers a glimmer of hope.

By SW5, Light openly challenges darkness. The Dark Side is still stronger, with a massive Imperial Fleet, an overwhelming attack on Hoth, and an overpowered Darth Vader dueling against his son. But the fleet can't catch the Millennium Falcon, the Hoth attack is fruitless, and Luke stands a fight against Darth Vader both physically and mentally, eventually escaping.

SW6 brings us resolution between the two. The Light and Darkness of Luke and his father eventually merge into Light. The Emperor dies a rightful death, and Darth Vader sacrifices himself for his son out of love. The galaxy is freed from its oppression.

The theme arc can be explained in a simple thread.

Episode 1: The galaxy is dominated by the Light Side, but Darkness seeps in.
Episode 2: Darkness strives to take over and Light fights back.
Episode 3: Light is snuffed out and Darkness wins.
Episode 4: Darkness dominates, but Light emerges.
Episode 5: Light grows and fights against Darkness, which fights back.
Episode 6: Light beats Darkness, canceling each other out, bringing back a seemingly neutral galaxy.

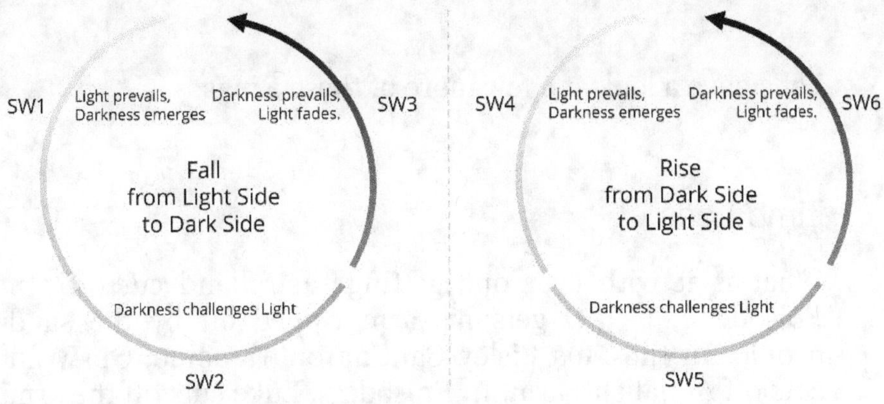

Figure 25 - Theme Rings in Star Wars 1 through 6.

Smaller Rings within the First Six Movies

The stories of the protagonists, the mentors, politics, and the theme are the main rings throughout the first six movies, but they are not the only rings. Ring Stories need to be fractal, such that many smaller rings pervade the movies. George Lucas made sure to embed rings and mirror images everywhere, from the grandiose scales of political systems, to the minute scale of details, such as their icons.

Figure 26 – Symbols of the Galactic Republic and the Galactic Empire. Even these are mirror images of each other!

Let's have a look at a few more of these Rings.

Limb Loss

What is it with everyone getting their hand cut off? In Episode 4, C-3PO gets his arm ripped off by the sand people. In the Mos Eisley Cantina on Tatooine, Obi-Wan cuts off Aqualish's arm. In Episode 5, Luke cuts off the arm of a Wampa in order to escape. The most remembered limb removal, however, is the mirror limb loss, when Luke loses his right hand to Darth Vader at the end of the movie. In Episode 6, Luke in turn cuts off Darth Vader's hand in a mirror action, realizing he had embarked on the Dark path too.

Episode 1 doesn't show any limb removal, but it does show Darth Maul being cut in half. I think that counts. Episode 2 features Obi-Wan cutting off Zam Wessell's arm when she attacks him in the bar. Then, Count Dooku cuts off Anakin's arm during their battle. This, of course, is the main limb loss mirroring Luke's.

Episode 3 brings us full circle with a whopper of limb loss. First, Count Dooku loses both hands to Anakin right off the bat. Then, Obi-Wan cuts off two hands of General Grievous. Anakin slices off Mace Windu's hand to protect Padmé. Then, for the finale, Obi-Wan unwillingly duels Anakin on the fiery volcano planet of Mustafar and cuts off Anakin's remaining human arm. Fueled by rage, Anakin attacks once more, forcing Obi-Wan to lop off all his remaining limbs. Physically and emotionally broken, Anakin suffers in pain, hatred, and anger. To add insult to injury, the lava seeps up next to him, catching his entire body on fire. At this time, we are all begging for mercy. Sure, he went Dark, but this is still Anakin, that innocent and misled boy from Tatooine. We know he turns into

Darth Vader, but what would we not give to put him out of his misery? This brings us to our next parallel.

Death, Birth, and Rebirth

At the end of SW3, Anakin is on the brink of death because of his injuries, and Padmé is close to death because of Anakin's choking, the pregnancy, and her broken heart.

At the end of Anakin's duel with Obi-Wan on Mustafar, we see Anakin screaming in anguish and pain, his flesh peeling away from the muscle underneath, veins exposed, and a mixture of melted fabric, skin, and blood dried on him. He is surrounded in a steamy dark room with rudimentary droids working on him. They slap metal limbs onto him with no regard to his comfort or the fact that he is dying. Here, time is all that matters.

This scene splits back and forth with Padmé. She is dressed in a hygienic white gown in a spotless, clean operating room. The droids are the latest technology, serene and seamless. Friends wait by her side, and her every need is met. During childbirth, she too screams in pain, and the twins are delivered safely. On their own, the two scenes are for the most part benign, but when they are spliced together the way Lucas did it, the emotions it renders are raw and contradictory. Anakin screams in pain for the path he took, and Padme screams in pain alone for the path Anakin took. What was supposed to be a blessing for the young couple is now a curse. What Anakin did to try and prevent Padme dying sealed her fate.

This is mirrored at the end of SW6. Instead of fighting for love, Luke renounces fighting for the same reason. He exposes himself to death in order to live morally. Anakin, suffering the mirror process of SW3, decides to lose his helmet to become human again and see his son for the first time with his own eyes, joining Padme in the celebration of the life of his child.

Deception of Vessels

Whenever a new character is introduced to the Millennium Falcon, they express confusion and frustration over how they are supposed to get away in a pile of junk ship. Han Solo naturally defends the honor of his prized ship, and even with some problems, the Millennium Falcon always seems to pull through (at least in the most crucial times, like battles and escaping). It appears the Millennium Falcon is deceptive. It looks like it can't do much, the interior is deteriorating, and there is always a part that needs replacing or rigging, yet it gets them through every time.

The Problem with C-3PO

R2-D2 and C-3PO follow a clear ring throughout the 6 episodes, meeting early on and then repeatedly splitting and meeting again.

But one ring that is particularly entertaining surrounds C-3PO alone. This protocol droid brags that he is fluent in over 6 million languages. He is timid and nervous in nature but possesses a vast wealth of knowledge. Despite all this knowledge, he is constantly talked over and second guessed. In almost every movie, with almost every character C-3PO interacts with, he is spoken over, not listened to, and underestimated. Sure, he is slightly annoying, but does it warrant the inattention? Symbolically, it shows the disregard for hard facts as a contrast with the Force's intuition. One of Han Solo's famous lines, directed at C-3PO, says: "Never tell me the odds." Even the Ewoks in Episode 6, though they regard him as a god, don't listen to him.

Also, C-3PO is never really complete. In Episode 1, he is merely parts. In Episode 2, he is fully assembled but not painted, and in the assembly line he is improperly assembled. In Episode 3, he is solid gold but he gets his mind wiped at the end. In Episodes 4–6, he has one silver leg. In Episode 5, he is blown to pieces (literally). And in Episode 7, he has an unmistakably red arm.

This echoes the use of robotic limbs for Luke and Anakin. They lose them in conflicts with the Dark Side, suggesting a connection between cybernetics and the Dark Side, as opposed to the very organic, intuitive Jedis.

The Recruitment Methods of the Light Side and the Dark Side

When it comes to the next generation of Siths or Jedis, there are some stark differences between the two. Palpatine was the original Sith in the first six movies, and is thus our only source of comparison. He would compel his apprentices to do his bidding without hesitation, and when they outlived their usefulness, he would sacrifice them to the next young apprentice: due to the Dark Side's Rule of Two, there can only be one master and one apprentice of the Dark Side at any given time.

Palpatine was always on the lookout for a younger, more powerful apprentice, often taking whatever means necessary to acquire more power. The Dark Side cycles through their Sith, pitting them against the older ones in a dog-eat-dog environment. This is evident when Palpatine faces Darth Maul against Jedis in SW1, when he encourages Anakin to kill Count Dooku in SW3, and when he forces Luke to go up against his father in SW6.

Conversely, Jedis also focus on only one padawan at a time, but they don't need to follow the Rule of Two. Every time they take a Padawan, they are very careful to train them and nurture them to develop them into new and powerful independent Jedis.

Next let's talk about how these rings and the Ring Structure can predict and has predicted the next three installments of the Star Wars Saga.

These are the main rings found within the Star Wars Movies Episodes 1 through 6. However, there are hundreds of smaller rings, parallels, similarities, and ironies throughout. It seems like every time we watch them again, we discover a new ring or parallel, and every time, the story structure becomes a little stronger. We could go on and on with rings, but that would take away your fun finding them!

Instead, let's turn our attention to the new installments, starting with Star Wars 7. Do they follow the Ring Structure?

Chapter 5: How the Ring Theory Predicted Star Wars VII – The Force Awakens

Episode 7 brought us a new protagonist, a new cast, and most of the old team again. It was a wonderful whirlpool of new situations in the usual theme, with a new varnish that only JJ Abrams, its creator, could provide – and not too many flares.

It pulled something off that is not easy to do. More than a decade after the last installment, Abrams had to overcome criticisms of Episodes 1-3, show that the new trilogy was going to go back to the roots of SW, and bring enough new elements to the table to refresh the saga.

Not many stories can pull this off. Think about all the Batman, Spiderman, Transformers, James Bond, or even Star Trek movies. Most stand on their own just fine, but there isn't much connecting them other than the same protagonist battling a different monster or bad guy in each film.

Instead, for SW7, Abrams was more ambitious.

Imagine you're him. You've grown up dreaming of lightsabers and Millennium Falcons. You've become one of the most powerful directors in Hollywood, known for your ability to breathe new life into anything you make. At the peak of your career, you are chosen to reboot one of the most beloved movie sagas in history. What do you do?

You start painstakingly studying every detail of the story. When you learn the ring structure, you structure your movie so that it widens the ring.

The Main Rings of SW7

The Protagonist Rings in SW1-4-7

Abrams had to establish first that this new trilogy was going to continue the ring saga of Star Wars. If SW 1-3 portray the rise of Anakin and SW 4-6 portray Luke's rise, the best way to show continuity was to make SW 7-9 the trilogy of Rey's rise. What better way than by espousing the parallels between Anakin, Luke, and Rey?

Star Wars 1 – The Phantom Menace	Star Wars 4 – A New Hope	Star Wars 7 – The Force Awakens
A poor boy lives in a broken family in a desert planet. He has great skills handling robots, and a special gift as a pilot.	A poor boy lives in a broken family in a desert planet. He has great skills handling robots, and a special gift as a pilot.	A poor girl lives in a broken family in a desert planet. She has great skills handling robots, and a special gift as a pilot.
Two representatives of the broader world appear in his life and shake his world: Qui Gon Jinn and Obi-Wan Kenobi.	Two representatives of the broader world appear in his life and shake his world: R2D2 and C3PO.	Two representatives of the broader world appear in her life and shake her world: Finn and BB-8.
The boy gets recruited with the promise of becoming a Jedi by his original Jedi mentor, Qui-Gon	The boy gets recruited with the promise of becoming a Jedi by his original mentor, Obi-Wan Kenobi.	The girl gets recruited by the original mentor, Han Solo. Han Solo has ties with the Light Side of the Force that she craves.

Jinn.		
The original mentor dies in a lightsaber fight with a Sith, and is replaced by a second mentor, Obi-Wan Kenobi.	The original mentor dies in a lightsaber fight with a Sith, and is replaced by a second mentor, Yoda.	The original mentor dies in a lightsaber fight with a Sith, and is replaced by a second mentor, Luke Skywalker.
The boy joins the Rebels and fights against the Dark Side.	The boy joins the Rebels and fights against the Dark Side.	The girl joins the Rebels and fights against the Dark Side.
A big enemy ship, the Trade Federation's, attacks the good guys' planet, Naboo.	A big enemy ship, the Death Star, attacks and destroys the good guys' planet, Alderaan.	A big enemy ship, the Starkiller Base, attacks and destroys the good guys' planets, the entire Hosnian system.
The boy is key in the destruction of the ship.	The boy is key in the destruction of the ship.	The girl is key in the destruction of the ship.

Figure 27 – Story parallels between SW1, SW4 and SW7.

Rey's story mirrors Anakin's and Luke's without a doubt. That's how it's clear that we're narrating a new ring of the saga.

The parallels don't stop here. They're not just about the protagonists. They are apparent across every ring.

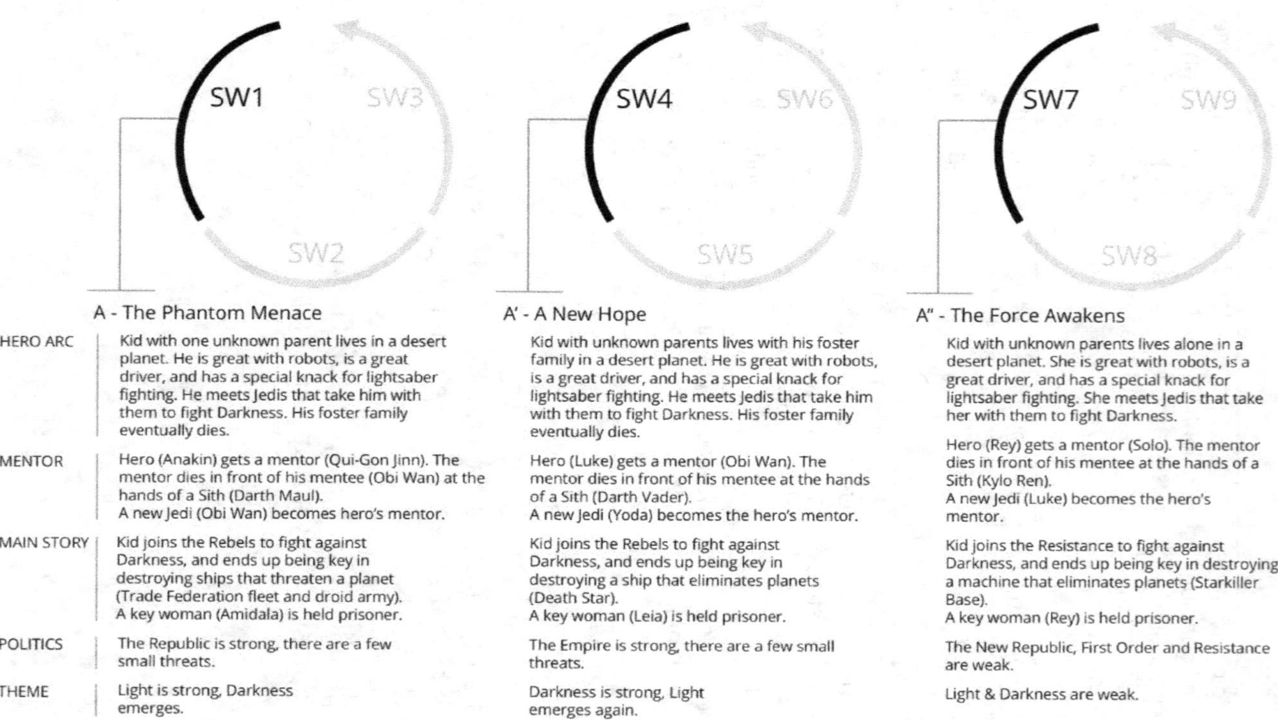

Figure 28 - Mirror Rings in Episodes 1, 4 and 7.

The Mentor's Ring

Just like Episodes 1 and 4, Rey's first mentor dies, and she must seek out a second mentor to teach her the ways of the Force. If there is any merit in the theory that, if a padawan witnesses their mentor dying, they will be strong in the Light Side of the Force, then the story is set for Rey to stay strong against the Dark Side. However, since Han Solo wasn't necessarily a Jedi mentor, the path isn't a particularly clear one. She goes on to locate a second mentor, Luke Skywalker, to teach her the ways of the Force.

Hopefully, the next two installments will expand on Kylo Ren's background. Since we know he turned to the Dark Side, is it possible he didn't witness his first mentor die? Maybe his first mentor is still alive; either way, it is a curious correlation of padawans witnessing their mentor's sacrifice and their path choices. In Episode 3, we hear the story of how Chancellor Palpatine/the Emperor killed his mentor in his sleep. He ended up being pure evil, and it wasn't even his father. What will happen to Kylo Ren in the coming Episodes after he murdered his own father? He did say he was having trouble and was being tempted. He asked for help from Han who agreed, thinking Kylo really meant he wanted help returning to the Light Side. Then, Kylo killed him, seemingly removing the temptation he was speaking of.

The Political Ring

As mentioned before, Episodes 1–6 show the pattern of the politics as follows:

Episode 1: The Republic is functional with very few threats.
Episode 2: The Republic has a growing threat that they attack preventatively.

Episode 3: The Republic falls and is tricked into allowing the Empire to rise.
Episode 4: The Empire is functional with very few threats.
Episode 5: The Empire has a growing threat that they attack preventatively.
Episode 6: The Empire falls, making way for a civil government to regain control.

Episode 7 picks up where Episode 6 leaves off. Both sides of the Force are stunted. The Dark Side is gaining headway with The First Order, by taking children from families and training them to be Stormtroopers. Its new head is Supreme Leader Snoke, and its second in command is Kylo Ren. The Light Side is more established, with a New Republic, and a new Resistance that is growing and continuing its efforts against the Dark Side.

The Theme Ring

The theme continues in this episode with the struggle between light and dark. Previously, each episode had the rise and fall of each side; Episodes 1–3 featured the Dark Side rising and taking over the galaxy, and Episodes 4–6 featured the Light Side rising to counter the effects of the Dark Side. In Episode 7, both sides are weak, fighting for supremacy.

It appears that Supreme Leader Snoke and Kylo Ren are the leaders of the Dark Side, and Rey and possibly Luke Skywalker are the representatives of the Light Side.

Episode 1: The galaxy is seemingly neutral, then darkness seeps in.
Episode 2: Darkness strives to take over and Light fights back.
Episode 3: Light is snuffed out and Darkness wins.
Episode 4: Darkness surrounds the galaxy but Light emerges.

Episode 5: Light grows and fights against Darkness.
Episode 6: Light and Dark cancel each other out, bringing back a seemingly neutral galaxy.
Episode 7: Both sides are weak but growing in power: Rey and Kylo; Resistance and First Order.

Smaller Rings in Episodes 1 through 7

BB-8 and Poe; R2D2 and Luke

There is a clear connection between pilot and droid. Anakin and R2D2 went through many battles together. Luke and R2D2 went through many as well. Now we see in this last trilogy with Poe and BB-8. Plus, these droids carried important information for the Rebels and Rebellion respectively. Both droids have quirky and eccentric personalities.

Jedi Mind Tricks

In SW2, we see Obi-Wan use his Jedi mind tricks on a bar patron. He tried to sell something called Death Sticks. Obi-Wan replies with "You want to go home and rethink your life", which the man repeats and leaves. Next, we see Luke use his power in Episode 6 to Bib Fortuna. Luke makes Bib tell Jabba that he will be allowed to speak. Obi-Wan uses his mind tricks again in possibly the most mimicked and remembered line of the Star Wars movies, "These aren't the droids you are looking for" and "He can go about his business; move along." Now, in this new Episode, The Force Awakens, after Rey realizes she can look into Kylo Ren's mind, she flexes her Jedi muscles a bit more. She tells the First Order Guard to "remove these restraints and leave with the cell door open", which fails the first time, but after believing in herself a bit more, her influence works, to her surprise.

Cantina Scenes

There are a few bar scenes in the movies, but two of them are outstandingly similar. The bar in Maaz Kanata's castle is introduced in SW7. It relies on very similar cinematics to those in the Mos Eisley Bar scene in Episode 4. Both cantinas are filled with a medley of aliens, droids, and human patrons, a dark setting with a comfortable and private feel, lively music, and shifty characters in an under-the-radar pit stop for space pirates. Another bar-like scene comes to mind as well. Jabba's lair has the same type of lively music surrounded by shifty characters and a wide range of humans, droids, and aliens. There is also a bar scene in Episode 2 where Anakin and Obi-Wan are looking for the Bounty Hunter trying to kill Padmé, although that one is much more cosmopolitan and rich. Maybe SW8 will have a new wealthy bar?

Desert Planets and the Skywalkers

We've already mentioned this a few times: Anakin was raised on the desert planet of Tatooine in a broken family, with his mother, where both were slaves. Luke was raised on the desert planet of Tatooine in a broken family, by his Step-Uncle and Step-Aunt, doing a job he isn't interested in doing. Rey didn't grow up in Tatooine, but her planet of Jakku is also a desert. She is in a broken family: alone, nearly enslaved, and by her flashbacks either a family or someone similarly close left her there. If the Skywalker line and orphaned upbringing on desert planets has any merit, then it is safe to say that Rey (especially with her already growing abilities) is a Skywalker... somehow. If she isn't literally a Skywalker, she is one by inheritance.

Death Spheres

It appears the Dark Side is obsessed with spherical Death Space Stations. It created the Death Star in Episode 4 and started rebuilding in the following Episodes, but slightly bigger. In Episode 7, they built a Starkiller Base from an ice planet in an unknown system. The sphere shape keeps coming up in the Dark Side's choice of planet-destroying weapons systems.

Blow-Up Scenes

Episodes 1, 4, 6, and 7 all include an epic blow-up scene with the good guys flying away from the destroyed ship in celebration.

Episode 1: Anakin unintentionally blows up the control ship and flies away.
Episode 4: Death Star 1 is blown up, and Luke and the Rebels fly away.
Episode 6: Death Star 2 blows up, followed by a fly away scene.
Episode 7: The Rebels blow up the Starkiller Base and fly away.
Episode 3 also has explosions, but they are too frequent to count.

The Sequel Trilogy follows the Original Trilogy

Abrams clearly established SW7 as the continuation of the saga. He used the story to do so, but he also used cinematics to achieve this continuity.

As in every other SW movie, the very first shot shows a scrolling text intro, or opening crawl, on a starred background. The camera pans down. Immediately, the movie turns away from the prequel trilogy with a shot of two planets and a star cruiser. This is the same beginning as movies 4, 5, and 6. But it's different from 1, 2 and 3. Was JJ trying to tell us something?

Indeed, he wanted to establish that the new movies would adhere much more closely to the original ones than the prequels did. Let's look into that.

SW7 is a new ring of SW4

Abrams wanted SW7 to mimic SW4 most closely among the films of the original trilogy. It's not just that the protagonists are similar. The entire movie is structurally identical to SW4.

Star Wars 4 – A New Hope	Star Wars 7 – The Force Awakens
Leia introduces a secret into a small rolling droid that doesn't speak, R2D2.	Poe Dameron introduces a secret into a small rolling droid that doesn't speak, BB-8
Darth Vader and his Stormtroopers chase the droid to find the secret. They kill everybody on their way and take a prisoner to find the secret, Leia.	Kylo Ren and his Stormtroopers chase the droid to find the secret. They kill everybody on their way and take a prisoner to find the secret, Poe.
We discover a young desert boy, Luke, who works with droids in a life he hasn't chosen.	We discover a young desert girl, Rey, who works with droids in a life she hasn't chosen.
Leia tries to resist Darth Vader's interrogation and succeeds. Vader decides to chase the droid.	Poe tries to resist Kylo Ren's interrogation but fails. Kylo decides to chase the droid. Rey tries to resist Kylo Ren's interrogation and succeeds.
A couple of partners, R2D2 and C-3PO, land on the desert planet.	A couple of partners, Poe and Finn, land on the desert planet.

The desert boy, Luke, stumbles upon a droid, R2-D2.	The desert girl, Rey, stumbles upon a droid, BB-8.
Luke is tempted by the Rebellion, but wants to remain on the desert planet because he has duties there.	Rey is tempted by the Resistance, but wants to remain in the desert planet because she has duties there.
The Millennium Falcon is dysfunctional, but the droid, Luke, and Solo use it to escape in extremis the attack of Stormtroopers.	The Millennium Falcon is dysfunctional, but the droid, Rey, and Finn use it to escape in extremis the attack of Stormtroopers.
The crew plays a chess game.	The crew retrieves the same chess game.
Luke receives Anakin's lightsaber.	Rey receives Anakin's lightsaber.
The crew goes to a cantina full of outcasts in Mos Eisley.	The crew goes to a cantina full of outcasts in Maz Kanata's castle.
The Millennium Falcon's controls are overridden by another ship. It gets captured.	The Millennium Falcon's controls are overridden by another ship. It gets captured.
A very old man, the Emperor, is at the head of the Dark Side and drives his black-hooded Sith, Darth Vader.	A very old human figure, Snoke, is at the head of the Dark Side and drives his black-hooded Sith, Kylo Ren.
The Death Star destroys a planet to show its power.	Starkiller Base destroys five planets to show its power.
The ship's crew witnesses how the young Jedi mentor, Obi-Wan, dies facing a Sith, Darth Vader.	The ship's crew witnesses how the young Jedi mentor, Solo, dies facing a Sith, Kylo.
The Death Star is destroyed with a master shot from an ace pilot, Luke.	Starkiller Base is destroyed with a master shot from an ace pilot, Poe.

Figure 29 – Scene by scene comparison of SW4 and SW7.

It's quite a statement to make the movie so similar to SW4! And keep virtually no other parallel with SW1's scenes. No pod racing, no blockade like the one against Naboo, no land attack, no droids, no underwater civilization, no senate... Abrams clearly wanted his movie to be associated with SW4 and not so much with SW1. He also used the Antagonist ring for the same purpose.

The Antagonist Ring

SW1 starts with the Trade Federation and its droids as the only antagonist, defeated by the end. Only in the subsequent movies do we discover who is the true antagonist, Palpatine / the Emperor.

SW7 avoids that. Instead, it mirrors SW4 much more closely. The new Empire is the First Order, with its Stormtroopers, its black and white colors with red accents, its star cruisers, and its planet-destroying weapons. It does add some new touches, like Stormtroopers who aren't clones, iconography reminiscent of Nazi Germany's Third Reich, and a completely new icon for the First Order – which, story-wise, makes sense: the First Order would want to reuse the weapons it inherited, but it would want to look different from the Empire. It wouldn't want to be associated with a failed project.

The new Emperor is Snoke, another Sith who also looks like a very, very old human, about whom we learn very little through the movie.

Finally, the new Darth Vader is Kylo Ren. Both are tall, dress in black, with a black helmet and a cape. Both are Skywalkers who choke people, read minds, and use their lightsabers within the first movie. SW1's Darth Maul does none of this. He just fights really well.

The New Ring

When we look at the 7 movies as a whole, we see that SW7 continues SW1 and SW4 in the rings of the hero, the mentor, the theme and the politics. But SW7 mirrors only SW4 in the details of the story and the antagonist's ring. Why did Abrams decide to pick up the rings, but remain closer to SW4 than SW1? There are two main reasons why.

First, he wanted to show that his movie was not only going to be a Star Wars movie, but one closer to the original trilogy than the prequels. Everybody wanted to distance themselves from the prequels. They had been badly criticized for drifting away from the spirit of Star Wars. Abrams wanted to tell us "No worries, the Star Wars you grew up loving is back".

The second reason was to kick-start the new ring of the saga. He needed to create new characters to tell a new story. He had to add something different to tell. But Anakin's ring was exhausted. We had already seen him rise and fall. We had already seen the Empire rise and fall, Darth Sidious rise and fall. And so, he created Rey to embody the new Ring.

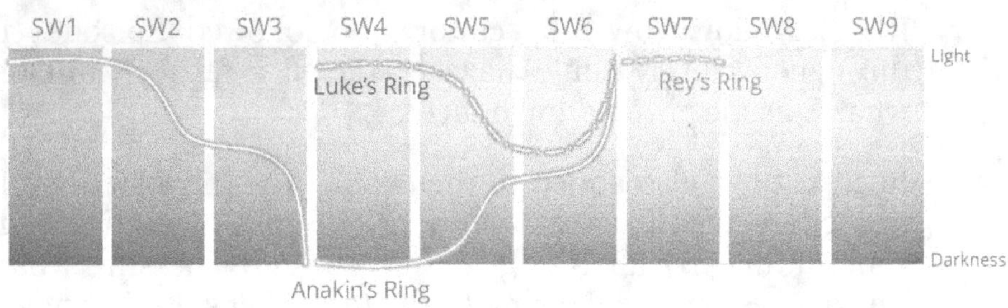

Figure 30 - Rings of Anakin, Luke and Rey.

Stacking the three rings shows their similarity.

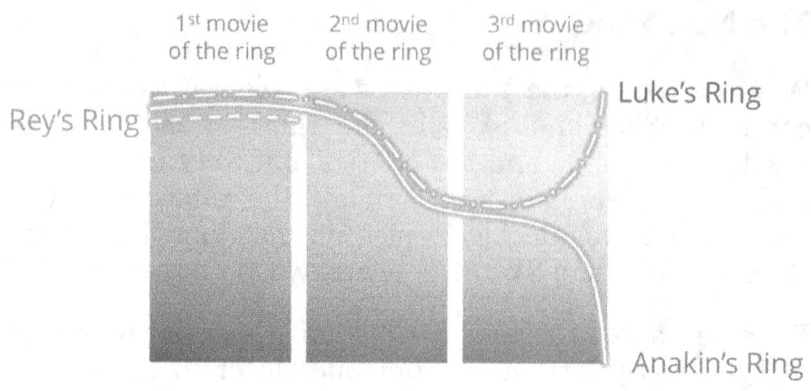

Figure 31 - Rings of Anakin, Luke and Rey, stacked.

SW7 started a new trilogy with one Ring exhausted (Anakin's), one Ring half-way through (Luke's) and one new Ring (Rey's). All thee start identically. By closely following SW4 with SW7, Abrams is telling us: "The new trilogy will close the ring of the original trilogy. It will close the story of Luke, Leia, and Solo. It will close their rise and fall, the way the original trilogy closed the prequels. And it will hand it off to the next generation."

It's clear now how a spectator who followed Episodes 1 through 6 closely could have predicted a fair amount of what Episode 7 would introduce.

But SW7 has also added to the canon. The introduction of new characters like Rey, Kylo Ren or Snoke have triggered a new Ring. By analyzing it, we can start guessing what Episodes 8 and 9 will bring to the table. Let's do that now.

Chapter 6: How the Ring Theory Predicts Star Wars 8 and 9

The legacy of Episode 7 is twofold. First, it has telegraphed to the audience that the SW7-9 ring will follow the pattern of rings, and specifically continue the SW4-6 rings, giving us a good sense of the storytelling structure for all movies.

Second, it introduces many new elements to imbue new life in the new rings. Who are Rey's parents? What has Luke been up to all these years? Why did he run away? Why did Kylo Ren turn to the Dark Side? How did it happen? How does Supreme Leader Snoke fit into all of this? Why does C-3PO have a red arm?

Let's see how each of these points can help us predict and understand what Episodes 8 and 9 will bring us.

2-5-8

Since the new trilogy is a new ring, Episode 8 will follow the main story elements of Episodes 2 and 5. What are they?

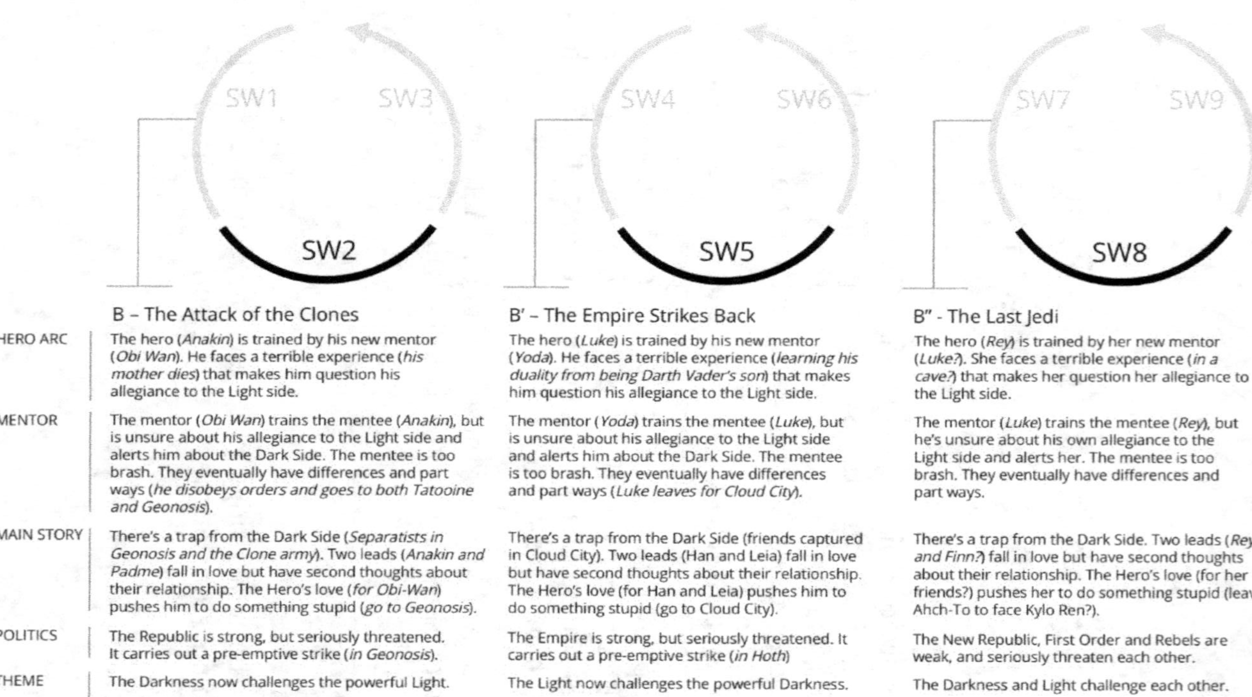

	B – The Attack of the Clones	B' – The Empire Strikes Back	B" - The Last Jedi
HERO ARC	The hero (*Anakin*) is trained by his new mentor (*Obi Wan*). He faces a terrible experience (*his mother dies*) that makes him question his allegiance to the Light side.	The hero (*Luke*) is trained by his new mentor (*Yoda*). He faces a terrible experience (*learning his duality from being Darth Vader's son*) that makes him question his allegiance to the Light side.	The hero (*Rey*) is trained by her new mentor (*Luke?*). She faces a terrible experience (*in a cave?*) that makes her question her allegiance to the Light side.
MENTOR	The mentor (*Obi Wan*) trains the mentee (*Anakin*), but is unsure about his allegiance to the Light side and alerts him about the Dark Side. The mentee is too brash. They eventually have differences and part ways (*he disobeys orders and goes to both Tatooine and Geonosis*).	The mentor (*Yoda*) trains the mentee (*Luke*), but is unsure about his allegiance to the Light side and alerts him about the Dark Side. The mentee is too brash. They eventually have differences and part ways (*Luke leaves for Cloud City*).	The mentor (*Luke*) trains the mentee (*Rey*), but he's unsure about his own allegiance to the Light side and alerts her. The mentee is too brash. They eventually have differences and part ways.
MAIN STORY	There's a trap from the Dark Side (*Separatists in Geonosis and the Clone army*). Two leads (*Anakin and Padme*) fall in love but have second thoughts about their relationship. The Hero's love (*for Obi-Wan*) pushes him to do something stupid (*go to Geonosis*).	There's a trap from the Dark Side (friends captured in Cloud City). Two leads (Han and Leia) fall in love but have second thoughts about their relationship. The Hero's love (for Han and Leia) pushes him to do something stupid (go to Cloud City).	There's a trap from the Dark Side. Two leads (*Rey and Finn?*) fall in love but have second thoughts about their relationship. The Hero's love (for her friends?) pushes her to do something stupid (leave Ahch-To to face Kylo Ren?).
POLITICS	The Republic is strong, but seriously threatened. It carries out a pre-emptive strike (*in Geonosis*).	The Empire is strong, but seriously threatened. It carries out a pre-emptive strike (*in Hoth*)	The New Republic, First Order and Rebels are weak, and seriously threaten each other.
THEME	The Darkness now challenges the powerful Light.	The Light now challenges the powerful Darkness.	The Darkness and Light challenge each other.

Figure 32 – Parallels between Episodes 2, 5, and 8.

5 is 8

As we say, it's not just that SW1, 4, and 7 are akin to each other, but that SW7 is much closer to SW4 than to SW1. It follows that SW8 will be like SW2 and SW5, but much closer to SW5 than SW2. What does that mean?

The Rey Ring

We know now that SW8 will follow SW2 and 5. What does that mean for the Rings of Luke and Rey?

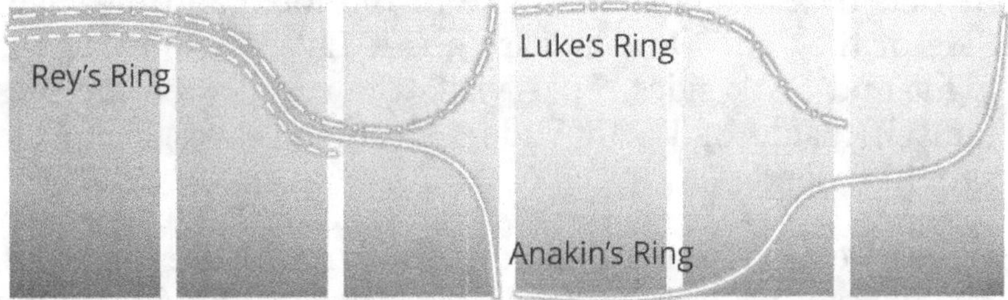

Figure 33 – Stacked Rings of Anakin, Luke and Rey, with a prediction for SW8 (dashed on the 2nd column for Rey and 5th for Luke).

Luke didn't end up on the Dark Side of the Force like his father. Similarly, Rey is not condemned to follow the same arc as Anakin or Luke. She is another stanza of the same song, one with its own rhyme.

Yet it's pretty clear, at least for SW8, that Rey will follow the Rings of both Anakin and Luke, while Luke will follow the mirror image of Anakin's Ring. That means that through SW8 - *The Last Jedi*, we will witness experiences that bring Rey and Luke to question Light and Darkness. What can these experiences be?

For some reason, Rey was abandoned to near-slavery on the desert planet of Jakku. Who did it? Was it her parents? Who are they? Why did they allow it? This childhood trauma is new; it adds a depth that no other ring had. This is what ties Rey to her world, why she doesn't want to leave the Ordinary World. The only thing that defines her is the people who left her behind. If she leaves that, who is she? This is likely to haunt her in the movies to come, until she fully overcomes it. That said, this might be just a light plot device: for a person who absolutely "has to go home", she is doing a lot of interstellar fighting and traveling in SW7…

The last shot of SW7 captures Rey handing Luke Skywalker his lightsaber. They are in Ahch-To, a very humid planet where the last known Jedi is secluded. This is exactly like Luke when he visits Yoda in the swampy Dagobah in SW5. At that time, Yoda trains Luke in the force and the Light Side of the Jedi. Doubts arise about Luke's affinity to the Light and Dark sides. Luke visits the cave, where he sees himself inside of Darth Vader. He then leaves hastily to save his friends.

We can expect something very similar with Rey in SW8. She will get training in the Force. Since SW8 will contain the Midpoint of the entire trilogy, she will have a cave experience that brings her a key insight about herself. Because of the rings of Light vs. Darkness, it is likely that this insight will question her allegiance to the Light Side.

The trailer shows indications of such a training, with Rey levitating rocks like Anakin in SW2's Coruscant and Luke in SW5's Dagobah. She also leaves a cave breathless, pointing to a Midpoint experience similar to Luke's. Whatever happens in the middle of the movie will be the key to unlock the entire trilogy. Where Anakin loses his mother and claims he wants to eliminate death in SW2, Luke saw his face in Vader's helmet and started doubting which side to pick in SW5. What will be Rey's Midpoint?

Since her main trauma is the fact that she was abandoned as a kid, and since both Anakin's and Luke's Midpoints refer to the family, Rey's cave experience will probably address her filiation.

Close to the end of SW7, when Kylo Ren tries to attract Luke's blue lightsaber, it ends up going to Rey. That probably means she is the rightful owner, so she may be Luke's daughter.

There is also a strong development of love stories in SW2 (Anakin and Padmé) and SW5 (Leia and Solo). If there is any love story in SW8, it might be between Rey and Finn, who had great chemistry in SW7. This would mirror especially Solo and Leia's story around the same time in the original trilogy. Remember that they kiss for the first time in a living-asteroid-cave in SW5. Rey might learn something about Finn or her love for him, pushing her to leave Ahch-To—hastily.

When Rey flies back to help her friends, she will probably encounter Kylo again, as Luke encountered Vader before her. If the ring is followed literally, Rey might lose a limb like Luke and Anakin before her. The limb loss is usually presented like a loss of humanity: in both cases, a natural limb is replaced by a machine limb in a step towards the Dark Side. This might symbolize Rey's move towards the Dark Side. If she doesn't have a limb cut, it might mean she is not influenced by the Dark Side at all.

The Luke Ring

Luke was attracted to the Light Side and the Dark Side, but at the end of SW6 he didn't fully embrace the Jedi path. It's not just the Emperor that wanted Luke to kill Vader. Yoda and Obi-Wan also told him he would have to do it. But Luke decided to follow a third path: stand down and use love to turn his father. It is closer to the Light side, but not the interpretation of the Light Side by other Jedis of the time.

The scriptwriters of SW8 and SW9 have probably reached this point and wondered: how do I add interest to the new sequel trilogy? How do I transform expectations and push characters to uncomfortable places? For Luke, they can push the movies in many directions, but a couple of them stand out.

It is possible that Luke's full ring is to bring balance to the Force. Where his father went from nothing to Dark Side to Light Side, Luke has gone from nothing to Light side, to bring Balance. Now, after trying and failing to rebuild the Jedis with a school for children, it is likely that he will try another way, one that isn't the way traditional Jedis have used the Light. He might try to extinct Jedis as we know them so that both sides of the Force can merge together and bring balance. And, like his father before him, he will probably succeed at his moment of death, probably at the end of SW9 if he follows Anakin's ring.

Another possibility is that his story is the mirror image of his father's. If Anakin ended up going from Dark Side to Light Side, Luke might go from Light Side to Dark Side. That would mean that Luke has turned, or will turn through the sequel trilogy. This would explain two things: why the logo of SW8 is the first one that's red, and why Luke's face in the movie's poster is red like Kylo Ren's, while Rey breaks through both their faces with a lightsaber that represents the symbol of the Jedi.

It may be that, when Luke explored the origin of the Jedi, he stumbled on them and also the origins of the Dark Side, and he believes the Dark Side to be misunderstood and more valuable than the Light Side. Maybe one of the ways this turn translates into the plot is that Luke will deny his help to his traditional friends, and Leia might die as a result.

The Kylo Ren Ring

Adding Kylo Ren to the mix adds an even more interesting hypothesis. One of the big novelties in this trilogy is that we don't see the development of just one young character. We see two: Rey and Kylo Ren. As Abrams put it, "Long before we had this title, the idea of The Force Awakens was that this would become the evolution of not just a hero, but a villain. And not a villain who was the finished, ready-made villain, but someone who was in process."

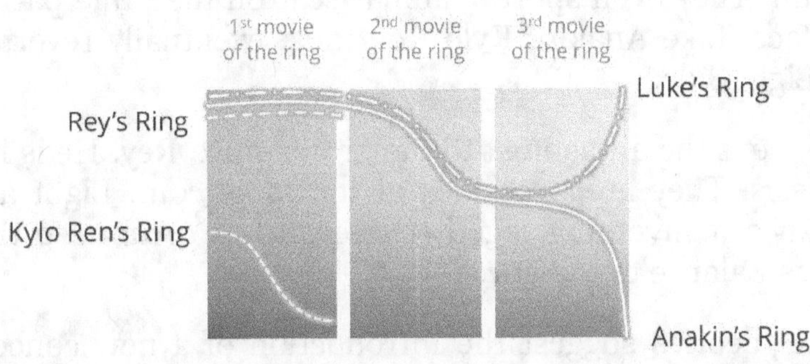

Figure 34 - Kylo Ren's Ring is unlike any other. Instead of starting stable on the light side, it starts in doubt and turns to the Dark Side when he kills his father, Han Solo.

Kylo Ren is probably the most interesting character in any first movie of a Star Wars trilogy.

Anakin in SW1, Luke in SW4, and Rey in SW7 are all nice, young people discovering the Force. It takes a full movie and a half for them to start doubting between the Light and Dark Sides. For Anakin, it's when his mother dies, and for Luke, when he sees himself in Darth Vader's helmet in the Dagobah cave.

Instead, Kylo Ren starts SW7 already doubting between both sides. You can see his insecurity and his rage as he deals with the doubt. In one of the final scenes, we see him ask for help from his father, Han Solo. His face, one side bathed in blue light, the other in red, shows the internal conflict, like Luke's fight at the end of SW6. But just when Solo is reaching to his soul, Starkiller Base fully sucks all the light out of the sun. The blue light that was bathing his face disappears. Red takes over Kylo's face, and the fate of his father is sealed.

This turn to the Dark Side can only be transient. Kylo Ren's full Ring must be one of redemption: he is like Anakin, a powerful Jedi turning to the Dark Side. He looks up to his grand-father. His worst fear is that he doesn't measure up to him. They even sport a similar scar on the same part of the face. Like Anakin, Kylo Ren must eventually revert to the Light Side.

Also, he is the antagonist to the protagonist, Rey. He is her nemesis. They are two sides of the same coin. Light and Darkness converging together... towards a *gray area* that brings Balance to the Force.

Some theories suggest the introduction of a new concept into the movies, *Gray Jedis*. The Ring structure predicts that something like this is highly likely, either literally Gray Jedis or something like that, where both sides are more nuanced. If we believe this, Luke might be the standard bearer of this new type of Jedi.

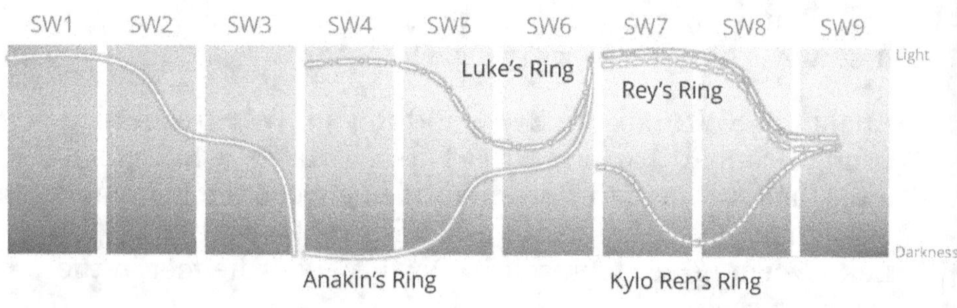

Figure 35 - Since Rey needs to move to a gray area in SW8, and Kylo Ren is Rey's nemesis, it is probable that Kylo Ren will move towards a gray area too in SW8 or SW9.

As a result of the Rings of Luke, Rey and Kylo Ren, it's likely that at the end of SW8, all three main characters will converge towards the middle gray area.

What other predictions can we make? A key factor in Kylo Ren's Ring, is Snoke, so we need to understand that Ring. Snoke is the new Emperor. He is training Kylo Ren, but he's eyeing Rey. It's like the Emperor, who trained Vader while eyeing Luke. In SW8, he will train Kylo Ren and expose him to further challenges to make him grow. Meanwhile, he will still try to find the map to Luke, so he can kill him and extinguish the Jedis.

His course of action will thus probably be to train Kylo Ren and ask him to chase the Resistance, who will probably be hiding in a desert planet like Hoth. We might even get a surface attack with Imperial Walkers or AT-ATs!

This is probably where Captain Phasma will enter the picture, leading or supporting the surface storm trooper attack. The trailer for Episode 8 shows a short scene of Poe and BB-8 racing down a hallway, very much like Solo and R2 racing the ice tunnels of Hoth. Poe is in his flight gear, and his plane explodes, pointing to another narrow escape much like the scenes in Episode 5 and the base on Hoth.

Snoke, General Hux, and Kylo will then use what they find there to attract Luke or Rey, or they might chase the crew until they can use something against Luke and Rey. They might use a fleeing Finn, who is sorely hurt at the end of SW7 and might be plunged into a bacta suit to revive at the beginning of SW8, much like Luke was in a bacta suit at the beginning of SW5. More likely, Finn and Poe should be able to escape and be chased by the First Order, like Han Solo, Leia, Chewy and C-3PO were in SW5.

Finally, if Kylo is the mirror image of Rey, like her, he might also lose a limb in SW8.

The Leia Ring

Another person Snoke and Kylo might use to force Rey and Luke to come to them is Leia. If SW7 focused on Solo as the member of the old guard, SW8 will focus on Luke, given how SW7 ends, and given the title of SW8: "The Last Jedi".

The logical next step would have been SW9's focus on Leia, but unfortunately this won't be possible given Carrie Fisher's death. Producers have said they won't use CGI to bring her back in SW9. That leaves them few options but to kill her in SW8. This might be a test that Kylo Ren must pass, which would leave Luke to die at the end of SW9. If Kylo Ren does indeed kill his mother in SW8, it might be the experience that sows more doubts in him with regards to the Dark Side.

Finn's Ring

Poe Dameron is an ace pilot, but beyond that he doesn't have a strong story arc. We can expect him to continue to embody the role of ace pilot.

We can't say the same of Finn. He started as a boy captured and indoctrinated by the First Order. After suffering from PTSD in his first battle, he can only think of escaping as far away as he can. At the Midpoint of SW7, he leaves Rey to escape, before realizing what is happening and turning around to save her.

His arc will probably continue through the next 2 movies. One possibility is a love arc with Rey, echoing the Solo-Leia love arc. However, the makers of SW8 have said love does not play a major role in the movie.

Another arc could be Finn overcoming his fear of the First Order and starting to fight for the Resistance. He might even try bringing the First Order down, perhaps becoming an inspirational figure for other Stormtroopers.

Linked to this is the fact that he is the first non-Jedi or Sith we ever see handling a lightsaber in a battle. And he held his own against Kylo, a Sith. Even if Kylo was wounded, Finn fights him for long enough that we might wonder if he has something to do with the Force.

Cloud City

SW5 is broadly divided in thirds: Hoth, Asteroids/Dagobah, and Cloud City. We've talked about the equivalents of Hoth – the desert planet where the Resistance is probably hidden – and Dagobah – Ahch-To, where Luke will train Rey –but not Cloud City. If SW8 uses the same planet structure as SW5, what will replace it?

The makers of SW8 have talked about a new planet called Canto Bight, a place full of wealth and opulence. The pictures of that place feature Leia, Poe, BB-8 and Finn, strengthening the likelihood that they escape together to this place. The arrival of newly-casted Benicio del Toro as DJ increases the probability that this is a place of debauchery and treachery, like Cloud City in SW5 or Coruscant in SW2. It would be a perfect setting for a bounty hunter, like the ones that appear both in SW2 and SW5.

The Light and Darkness Ring

Episodes 1–3 are the Thesis, Episodes 4–6 are the Antithesis, and Episodes 7–9 are to be the Synthesis. We should expect a resolution of the struggle between Light and Darkness.

Episode 7 set this up by demonstrating that both sides are weak, but growing in numbers and weapons. Episode 8, then, should build increasing tension between the two sides, gearing up for a final battle where everything is on the table. Episode 9 should increase the tension all the way up to the Climax, when Light and Dark Sides merge into Balance.

Bringing it all together

It's time to use everything we've discussed to predict what happens in SW8 and SW9.

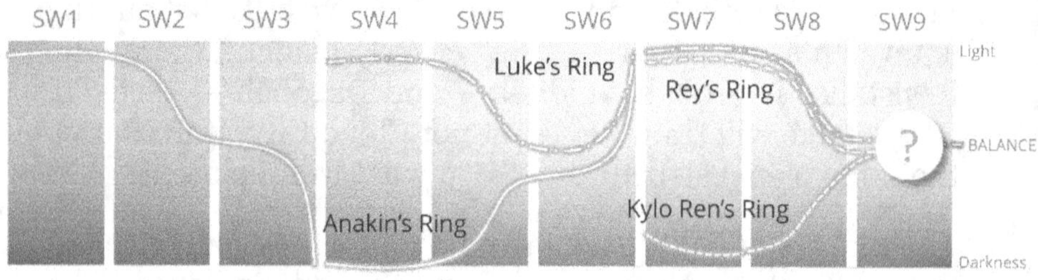

Figure 36 - Projection of the rings of Luke, Rey and Kylo Ren in Episodes 7 through 9.

Episode 8 opens. The theme of Light and Darkness is introduced in a secondary setting, maybe a desert planet where the Rebellion is hiding, like Geonosis in SW2 and Hoth in SW5. Crait is the biggest candidate for that.

Meanwhile, Luke and Rey discuss the Force and the Jedis in Ahch-To's island. Rey wants Luke to come and help the Resistance, and maybe train her, but they will have a disagreement. Luke will have begun to have doubts again about the Light and Dark Sides of the Force. If he has renounced the Jedi way, he may be unwilling to train another Jedi the way Jedis have been trained in the past.

Whether actively, through Jedi training, or passively, through the conflict between Light and Darkness, Rey will learn from Luke. He will share with her the knowledge he has been accumulating. During her training, Rey will wander into a cave, maybe attracted by the Force. In there, she will face some form or another of her own personal evil. That evil will probably be linked to her filiation, and will likely present a true fight between the Light Side and the Dark Side. Either at that point or later, Rey and the viewer need to learn more about Rey's origins. Then, as they near the end of Rey's training, she will leave prematurely to help her friends, maybe falling into a trap from Snoke and Kylo Ren. Luke will not want her to leave, but she will leave regardless.

Poe, Finn and Leia have their own personal struggles with the Dark Side. The Rebel base will be attacked, and Kylo Ren, Captain Phasma, or both will storm the base with the First Order. Poe, Finn, R2D2, and Leia will probably escape, but they will be used as bait regardless.

Captain Phasma, Kylo Ren, or Supreme Leader Snoke will hatch a plan to capture Rey and Luke. They will think they can turn her and destroy him. The trap might involve someone Rey loves, a family member we learn about, or even Finn. Even against Luke's advice, Rey will foolishly, but heroically, face the captors head on and fall into their trap.

This trap will probably drive her to a treacherous world with some sort of bounty hunter, like Coruscant in SW2 and Cloud City in SW5. There, she will end up facing Kylo Ren, where one or both might just lose a hand. Both will live to fight a final battle in Episode 9.

Kylo Ren will also face a new ordeal, and Leia will probably die. Both events might be connected, for a stronger impact to Kylo's character.

Episode 9 will feature the final battle between Light and Darkness, Rey and Kylo Ren, Luke and Snoke, but this one should end in a balanced galaxy and a balanced Force, instead of either Light or Dark Forces taking over. Luke will die, maybe by sacrificing himself for Rey, maybe after turning. Rey and Kylo Ren will represent two sides of the same coin, who will merge – figuratively – to find the Balance. Rey's filiation will be key.

By the end of this episode, we should also know how Kylo Ren turned and why he did it, what Luke was trying to do with the new type of Jedi, and what Balance looks like for the Force.

The force that should bring Balance between the Light and the Dark Sides is Love. For Anakin, it was love for his mother that brought him to anger, and love for Padmé that brought him to fear. For Luke, love of his friends brought him anger, and love for Leia brought him the fear of losing them. But eventually, love for his father was stronger and he overcome fear and anger. Similarly, it will be Love that brings Balance to the Force at the end of SW9 through Rey and Kylo Ren.

Conclusion

Rings are a storytelling technique that provide structure for some of the most ambitious and important stories in history. George Lucas discovered them as he was making his original trilogy, and decided to expand them to his new trilogy, forming a unique series of 6 movies guided by an intricate ring structure.

He passed the baton to Disney, but the spirit of what he accomplished lives on. JJ Abrams followed his steps in *Star Wars 7 – The Force Awakens*. We can expect Rings to be used in Episodes 8 and 9. It is impossible to predict what happens with precision, because Rings are like repeating stanzas of a song with different rhymes to them, but they enable us to understand and predict where the story will go.

But in the end, what should we take away from all of this? Why does this even matter? This isn't about fan fiction, or losing touch with reality. This is about appreciating one of the most ambitious sagas of cinema history.

Using Ring Structure is not a gimmick. Reusing the same themes with slight variations gives a sense of harmony to a story, like rhymes in poetry. Rings also reflect history, which repeats itself again and again, colored by the times.

The story that George Lucas wrote was not just another DVD in a collection, or just another box office hit. It was a story that utilized an ancient and highly revered storytelling method. He not only used the Ring Structure but also completely entwined countless themes and ideas throughout the entire saga. The level of forethought needed to create such a complex web of a story is staggering.

This structure is what has made Star Wars unique. It was ground-breaking at the time, attracting millions of fans. Since then, its impact has only grown because the movies don't age. They don't age because they're eternal, and they're eternal because the Ring structure impacts our subconscious like a work of poetry.

Much in the same way Da Vinci was praised for the Mona Lisa, or Van Gogh for his Starry Night, or F. Scott Fitzgerald for his book *The Great Gatsby*, we should appreciate Star Wars as a work of art whose ambition will inspire generations of storytellers. If there is anything that you take from this book, it should be to respect and appreciate the amount of work put into the Star Wars universe and how these films have changed popular culture since their release. As George himself once said:

"The interesting thing about Star Wars—and I didn't ever really push this very far, because it's not really that important—but there's a lot going on there that most people haven't come to grips with yet. But when they do, they will find it's a much more intricately made clock than most people would imagine."

—George Lucas to Vanity Fair in Feb. 2005

Young padawan, now that you're equipped with the insight of the Ring Structure, the next step is to go find your own rings yourself: in the Star Wars movies, trailers and articles, but also across other ambitious works of storytelling. Some of them may be weaker, some may be very strong, but now that you understand what Ring Theory is, don't be surprised if you find Rings everywhere!

I hope you enjoyed this book as much as I enjoyed writing it. If you found it useful in any way, a review on Amazon would be appreciated and would help others discover the book too! Thank you, and may the Force be with you.

APPENDIX

The following summary of every Star Wars movie can be used as a reference throughout the book, if there are details you've missed or you have forgotten about the movies.

The Original Trilogy

The Original Trilogy refers to the first three movies George Lucas made of Star Wars, between the end of the 1970s and the beginning of the 1980s. They are Episodes IV – A New Hope, Episode V – The Empire Strikes Back, and Episode VI –The Return of the Jedi.

Star Wars Episode IV – A New Hope

SW4 is the story of Luke Skywalker. He lives in a desert planet called Tatooine, and suddenly stumbles upon a robot, R2D2, with a secret message. The secret message is from a beautiful princess, Leia, asking for help from Obi-Wan Kenobi. Luke ends up going to see Obi-Wan, who asks him to join the Rebellion against the evil Empire that rules the galaxy.

Luke is initially reluctant, but when his foster family is killed by the evil Empire, he decides to join the Rebellion. He goes with Obi-Wan to a spaceport where they meet Han Solo and his companion Chewbacca. Together, they leave Tatooine to go meet princess Leia.

When they arrive to her planet, Alderaan, it's not there. The Empire just destroyed it with a new weapon, the Death Star. Our crew's ship is captured by that Death Star. Once inside, the crew escapes and frees princess Leia. As they are about to leave, Obi-Wan Kenobi confronts the evil Darth Vader and dies during the lightsaber fight.

Princess Leia leaves the Death Star with the rest of the crew and the plans on how to destroy the Death Star. They join the Rebellion, who prepares a suicide attack on the Death Star. They attack, but most ships are destroyed. Luke, one of the last survivors, suddenly uses what he's learned from Obi-Wan Kenobi, the Force, and shoots the Death Star in its only weak spot, destroying it.

Star Wars Episode V – The Empire Strikes Back

In SW5, the Empire retaliates against the Rebellion by attacking one of its bases. Everybody escapes. Luke sees a vision of Obi-Wan Kenobi, telling him to go to a planet called Dagobah to learn the Force from a Jedi master called Yoda. He follows that vision, and ends up with Yoda, training to become a Jedi.

Han Solo and Leia, together with their sidekicks Chewbacca and C-3PO, try to escape the Empire but they are chased, so they enter an asteroid field to escape. They land in a cave, which turns out to be a monster's throat. They escape and seek refuge with one of Han Solo's friend, Lando Calrissian. Unbeknownst to them, they are followed by the Empire, who makes them prisoners as a trap for Luke Skywalker.

Luke keeps training in Dagobah, but feels that his friends are in danger, so he drops everything and goes to save them. It is indeed a trap: Darth Vader is there. He faces Luke in another lightsaber fight and cuts his hand. Disarmed, he asks Luke to join him in the Dark Side. To convince him, he reveals him that he's his father. Luke doesn't want to believe it and jumps into the void, but his friends have escaped and save him.

The only member of the crew that's missing is Han Solo, who was frozen as a gift for a bounty hunter who helped the Empire find the crew.

Star Wars Episode VI – The Return of the Jedi

Luke, Leia, Chewbacca, Lando, C-3PO and R2D2 go to liberate Han Solo from his frozen prison. They go to the palace of a bandit leader, Jabba the Hut. They end up killing him, along with all his entourage, and free Han Solo.

Luke leaves to complete his training with Yoda. He learns from him, but Yoda soon dies, so Luke gathers again with the rest of his friends.

Meanwhile, the Empire is building another Death Star, so the Rebellion is planning another attack. They need to land on a planet called Endor's moon to disable its protecting shield, while a fleet is on standby to attack the Death Star as soon as it's unprotected.

The Rebellion lands on Endor's moon and captures the shield. Luke hands himself to the Empire, because he feels that his destiny is to confront his father, Darth Vader. Vader takes his son with him to the Death Star and discovers that Endor's moon is a trap. Hidden Empire forces take over from the Rebellion, so when the fleet of spaceships attack the Death Star, they realize they can't destroy it. At that point, a hidden Empire fleet arrives to destroy the Rebels' ships.

A local species in Endor, the Ewoks, attack the Empire to defend their friends the Rebels. That enables the Rebels to overtake the shield again and destroy it, leaving the Death Star unprotected.

Meanwhile, the Emperor is in the Death Star, trying to turn Luke to the Dark Side. The Emperor is the leader of the Rebellion; Darth Vader his powerful sidekick. The Emperor has sensed that Luke is very powerful and wants to make him his other sidekick. Luke refuses, so the Emperor starts killing him. Darth Vader, seeing that his son is about to die, turns against his Emperor and kills him.

Meanwhile, the Rebel ships take advantage of the Death Star's shield destruction to attack it. Before it explodes, Luke thanks his dad, who is terminally injured. Vader asks to take off his helmet to see his son for the first time. They reconcile, Luke leaves, and the Death Star gets blown up again.

The Prequel Trilogy

The Prequel Trilogy refers to the three movies George Lucas made at the end of the 1990s and beginning of the 2000s. They are Episode I – The Phantom Menace; Episode II – The Attack of the Clones; and Episode III – The Revenge of the Sith. They happen around 30-40 years before Episode IV.

Episode I – The Phantom Menace

Planet Naboo is blockaded by the Trade Federation. Jedis Obi-Wan Kenobi and his master Qui-Gon Jinn go in a diplomatic mission to handle the situation.

Darth Sidious, a Sith Lord like Darth Vader and the Emperor in the Original Trilogy, orders the Federation to kill the Jedi and invade Naboo, but the Jedi escape to Naboo. They meet Jar Jar Binks, a local outcast from the species Gungan, who leads the Jedi to the underwater Gungan capital. The Jedi try to persuade the Gungan leader to help the people of Naboo, but he doesn't accept. The Jedi leave the Gungan city and travel back to the surface, where they rescue the local Queen Amidala, the ruler of the Naboo people. They all escape the planer, but their ship is damaged so they end up seeking repairs in the desert planet of Tatooine, the same one as Luke Skywalker's.

There, they meet a nine-year-old slave, Anakin Skywalker, a gifted pilot and engineer, and eventual father of Luke and Leia. Qui-Gon senses that the Force is strong in Anakin and thinks he is the "chosen one" who will bring balance to the Force. After a race won by Anakin, he gains freedom and leaves with Qui-Gon, Obi-Wan and Amidala for the capital planet of the Republic, Coruscant.

There, Amidala pleads for help from the Senate, but the ineffective Chancellor can't make it happen, so she makes a vote of no confidence under the advice of Senator Palpatine. It is successful but the Senate is still ineffectual, so she goes back to Naboo to handle the situation by herself.

Qui-Gon and Obi-Wan are ordered by the Jedi Council to go with her. They take Anakin with them as a new padawan (Jedi trainee), despite the Council's advice against it.

On Naboo, Amidala begs the Gungans for help, persuading them to help against the Trade Federation. A battle ensues. Anakin inadvertently joins the space part of the battle, and destroys the mothership, disabling the Trade Federation's droid army.

Meanwhile, Qui-Gon and Obi-Wan battle a sith lord called Darth Maul, who kills Qui-Gon before dying himself. In his deathbed, Qui-Gon asks Obi-Wan to train Anakin. Palpatine is elected as the new Supreme Chancellor. The Jedi Council promotes Obi-Wan to the rank of Jedi Knight and accepts Anakin as Obi-Wan's padawan.

Episode II – The Attack of the Clones

Ten years after the Trade Federation's invasion of Naboo, a Separatist movement led by Count Dooku threatens the Republic. Amidala, has taken the old Senator position of Chancellor Palpatine. She comes to Coruscant to vote on the creation of an army for the Jedi. She narrowly avoids two assassination attempts, so she goes back to Naboo, escorted by Anakin. Obi-Wan starts searching for the culprit behind the assassination attempts

Obi-Wan goes to the remote ocean planet Kamino, where an army of clones is being manufactured for the Republic. Bounty hunter Jango Fett serves as its genetic template. Obi-Wan believes Jango is behind the assassination attempts, so he follows him to desert planet Geonosis.

Meanwhile, Anakin and Padme start a love relationship, and Anakin starts having premonitions that his mother, Shmi, is in pain. He travels to Tatooine with Amidala to save Shmi, but he arrives too late. He finds her badly tortured in a Tusken campsite, so he massacres the Tuskens before claiming that he wants to prevent death.

On Geonosis, Obi-Wan discovers that Count Dooku leads the Separatist movement, has a droid army, and is behind the assassination attempt on Amidala. Obi-Wan transmits his findings to Anakin to relay to the Jedi Council, but is captured mid-transmission. Given the situation, the Senate votes emergency powers for Supreme Chancellor Palpatine to send the clones into battle against the droids. Anakin and Amidala go assist Obi-Wan, but are also captured and all sentenced to death.

The Jedis and their newly found clones come to the rescue, kill Jango, save the crew and start fighting the droid army. Anakin, Obi-Wan and Yoda pursue Dooku. He severs Anakin's arm before escaping to Coruscant to deliver the blueprint for the Death Star to Darth Sidious.

Anakin gets a robotic replacement for his lost limb and secretly marries Amidala.

Episode III – The Revenge of the Sith

The Galaxy has been at war for three years since the last movie. The Separatists led by Count Dooku and a robotic General Grievous kidnap Chancellor Palpatine in Coruscant, but Anakin and Obi-Wan free him. Anakin kills Count Dooku on Palpatine's orders, and General Grievous escapes.

Back in Coruscant, Anakin learns that Amidala is pregnant, and starts having dreams that she dies in childbirth.

Chancellor Palpatine and the Jedi Council ask Anakin to spy on each other, which puts him in a stressful situation. Obi-Wan is sent to kill General Grievous, which he does, and Yoda travels to protect a planet from Separatist invasion. While they, and most other Jedis, are away fighting the Separatists, Palpatine revels to Anakin that he is a Dark Lord and possesses the power to help people survive death.

Initially, Anakin reports this to the only Jedi Council member left in Coruscant, Mace Windu, who goes to arrest Palpatine. Anakin arrives at the scene right when Mace Windu is about to kill Palpatine. Surprised at the unethical behavior of Windu, and for fear of losing the only potential lifeline for Amidala, he cuts Mace Windu's arms and Palpatine, now revealed to be Darth Sidious, kills Windu. He then anoints Anakin as Darth Vader, his apprentice.

With the Separatist leaders dead, no Jedi Council members in Coruscant left, and most Jedis exposed in different battles across the Galaxy, Sidious orders his Clone armies to betray and kill all remaining Jedis. Only Obi Wan and Yoda are known to survive. While the clones kill all Jedis,

Anakin turned Darth Vader takes care of the younglings, children Jedi apprentices.

Sidious addresses the Senate, misrepresents the Jedi as a threat to the Republic, and declares the Empire to replace the Senate. Obi-Wan and Yoda return to face Vader and Sidious respectively.

Yoda confronts Sidious, but is unable to kill him and flees with Bail Organa, a senator for Alderaan. Obi-Wan secretly follows Amidala to find Vader, who was sent to dispose of the remaining leaders of the Separatist movement in a faraway planet called Mustafar. There, Darth Vader and Obi-Wan have a duel to death. Obi-Wan has the upper hand, cuts all of Vader's limbs, and leaves him to die burning close to the planet's lava rivers.

Sensing Darth Vader in danger, Darth Sidious sends for him and saves him. He builds him a special suit to keep him alive and replace his organic limbs with robotic ones.

Meanwhile, Obi-Wan regroups with Yoda just at the moment when she gives birth to twins, Leia and Luke, and dies. Resolved to keep them alive as the only hope of the galaxy, Bail Organa resolves to adopt Leia as his own daughter and brings her with him to Alderaan, while Obi-Wan takes Luke to a foster family in Tatooine, his father's homeland. He will keep an eye on the baby until the time comes to challenge the Empire.

The Sequel Trilogy

The Sequel Trilogy refers to the three new Star Wars movies, Episode VII – The Force Awakens, Episode VIII – The Last Jedi, and Episode IX. These movies have been produced under Disney, not under George Lucas's creative vision anymore.

Episode VII – The Force Awakens

Three decades after the destruction of the second Death Star and the fall of the Empire, the New Republic is weak, the First Order has risen from the ashes of the Empire, and the Resistance led by General Leia Organa has set to confront it. She looks for the help of Luke Skywalker, her brother, who is nowhere to be seen after his school for new Jedi children got destroyed, and all its younglings killed.

Poe Dameron, a Resistance pilot, arrives to the desert planet Jakku to obtain a map of Luke's whereabouts. Stormtroopers commanded by Kylo Ren capture Poe, but only after he hides the map in a small robot, BB-8. Ren tortures Poe and discovers the existence of the robot, so he sends a force to Jakku to capture the robot. Finn, a Stormtrooper that doesn't want to be one anymore, defects from the First Order and frees Poe to use him as his pilot. They steal a ship and crash on Jakku. Finn wakes up alone in the middle of the deserts and starts looking for human presence. He finds Rey, who found BB-8 and is hanging out with him. The three of them flee the planet just as the First Order attacks them.

Their ship is captured by a larger one piloted by Han Solo and Chewbacca. Unfortunately, they owe money to two rival gangs that board the ship to claim their dues. The new crew escapes, but they let the First Order know about the new development. At the First Order's Starkiller Base, a planet converted into a kind of super Death Star, the Supreme Leader of the First Order, Snoke, orders the use of the weapon for the first time.

The crew views BB-8's map, but find out it isn't complete. Looking for clues, they travel to the planet Takodana to meet Maz Kanata, who offers assistance in getting BB-8 to the Resistance. Rey is drawn to a vault on the lower level and finds the lightsaber that once belonged to Luke and his father, Anakin Skywalker. Maz tells her it belongs to her, but she flees. She gives it to Finn instead.

Starkiller Base finally attacks and destroys the New Republic's capital, along with four other planets and the main Republic fleet. The First Order attacks Takodana in search of BB-8. Kylo Ren finds Rey alone in a forest, discovers she has seen the map, and captures her thinking that he doesn't need the robot anymore. However, when he interrogates her in Starkiller Base, she resists his mind-reading attempts: she can use the Force too. She eventually escapes using a Jedi mind trick on a nearby guard.

At the Resistance base, all the other characters meet: Han Solo, Chewbacca, Leia, BB-8, Poe Dameron, Finn, C-3PO and R2D2, who is inoperative. They start planning an attack on Starkiller Base: Finn, Chewbacca, and Han Solo will disable the planet's shield, and Poe and his fleet will then attack its weak point.

The crew infiltrates the facility, finds Rey, and plants explosives. Han confronts Kylo, who is his son, but he kills his father. The crew detonates the explosives, disabling the shield and enabling Poe to destroy the planet's weakest point. Before that, Kylo confronts Finn, and then Rey, in a lightsaber fight. Rey wins and escapes with the rest of the crew. Snoke orders to evacuate Kylo.

Back with the celebrating resistance, R2D2 wakes up and reveals the rest of the map. Rey uses it to find Luke.

Endnotes

[i] Adrienne Lafrance, "The Six Main Arcs in Storytelling, as Identified by an A.I.", The Atlantic, 2016, https://www.theatlantic.com/technology/archive/2016/07/the-six-main-arcs-in-storytelling-identified-by-a-computer/490733/

[ii] Andrew J. Reagan, Lewis Mitchell, Dilan Kiley, Christopher M. Danforth, and Peter Sheridan Dodds, "The emotional arcs of stories are dominated by six basic shapes", University of Vermont, 2016, https://arxiv.org/pdf/1606.07772.pdf

[iii] Inspired by John Yorke, "Into the Woods", 2015

[iv] Anne Lancashire, "The Phantom Menace: Repetition, Variation, Integration", Film Criticism, 2000, https://www.thefreelibrary.com/The+Phantom+Menace%3A+Repetition,+Variation,+Integration-a065131412

[v] Scott Chernoff, "The Plot Thickens", Star Wars Insider, 2002

[vi] George Lucas, "The Beginning: Making Episode I", 2001

[vii] Mike Klimo, "Star Wars Ring Theory", 2014, http://www.starwarsringtheory.com/